Computing and Communications in the Extreme

Research for Crisis Management and Other Applications

Steering Committee
Workshop Series on High Performance Computing and Communications
Computer Science and Telecommunications Board
Commission on Physical Sciences, Mathematics, and Applications
National Research Council

NATIONAL ACADEMY PRESS
Washington, D.C. 1996

NOTICE: The project that is the subject of this report was approved by the Governing Board of the National Research Council, whose members are drawn from the councils of the National Academy of Sciences, the National Academy of Engineering, and the Institute of Medicine. The members of the steering committee responsible for the report were chosen for their special competences and with regard for appropriate balance.

This report has been reviewed by a group other than the authors according to procedures approved by a Report Review Committee consisting of members of the National Academy of Sciences, the National Academy of Engineering, and the Institute of Medicine .

Support for this project was provided by the Department of the Navy, Office of the Chief of Naval Research, under grant number N00014-93-1-0166. The project was conducted at the request of the Department of Defense, Defense Advanced Research Projects Agency. The content of this workshop report does not necessarily reflect the position or the policy of the federal government, and no official endorsement should be inferred.

Library of Congress Catalog Card Number 96-60885
International Standard Book Number 0-309-05540-7
Additional copies of this report are available from: National Academy Press 2101 Constitution Avenue, N.W. Box 285 Washington, DC 20055 800-624-6242 202-334-3313 (in the Washington Metropolitan Area)

Copyright 1996 by the National Academy of Sciences. All rights reserved.

Printed in the United States of America

On the cover: A photograph provided by the Federal Emergency Management Agency shows urban search and rescue workers in action at the Alfred P. Murrah Building in Oklahoma City, April 1995. A computer graphic produced by the Geophysical Fluid Dynamics Laboratory, National Oceanic and Atmospheric Administration, depicts a simulation of Hurricane Emily off the North Carolina Coast, September 1993.

STEERING COMMITTEE, WORKSHOP SERIES ON HIGH PERFORMANCE COMPUTING AND COMMUNICATIONS

KEN KENNEDY, Rice University, *Chair*
FRANCES E. ALLEN, IBM T.J. Watson Research Center
VINTON G. CERF, MCI Telecommunications
GEOFFREY FOX, Syracuse University
WILLIAM L. SCHERLIS, Carnegie Mellon University
BURTON SMITH, Tera Computer Company
KAREN R. SOLLINS, Massachusetts Institute of Technology

Staff

MARJORY S. BLUMENTHAL, Director
JAMES E. MALLORY, Program Officer (through April 1995)
JOHN M. GODFREY, Research Associate
GAIL E. PRITCHARD, Project Assistant

COMPUTER SCIENCE AND TELECOMMUNICATIONS BOARD

WILLIAM A. WULF, University of Virginia, *Chair*
FRANCES E. ALLEN, IBM T.J. Watson Research Center
DAVID D. CLARK, Massachusetts Institute of Technology
JEFF DOZIER, University of California, Santa Barbara
HENRY FUCHS, University of North Carolina
CHARLES GESCHKE, Adobe Systems Incorporated
JAMES GRAY, Microsoft Corporation
BARBARA GROSZ, Harvard University
JURIS HARTMANIS, Cornell University
DEBORAH A. JOSEPH, University of Wisconsin
BUTLER W. LAMPSON, Microsoft Corporation
BARBARA LISKOV, Massachusetts Institute of Technology
JOHN MAJOR, Motorola
ROBERT L. MARTIN, AT&T Network Systems
DAVID G. MESSERSCHMITT, University of California, Berkeley
WILLIAM H. PRESS, Harvard University
CHARLES L. SEITZ, Myricom Incorporated
EDWARD H. SHORTLIFFE, Stanford University School of Medicine
CASIMIR S. SKRZYPCZAK, NYNEX Corporation
LESLIE L. VADASZ, Intel Corporation
MARJORY S. BLUMENTHAL, Director
HERBERT S. LIN, Senior Staff Officer
PAUL SEMENZA, Staff Officer
JERRY R. SHEEHAN, Staff Officer
JEAN E. SMITH, Program Associate
JOHN M. GODFREY, Research Associate
LESLIE M. WADE, Research Assistant
GLORIA P. BEMAH, Administrative Assistant
GAIL E. PRITCHARD, Project Assistant

COMMISSION ON PHYSICAL SCIENCES, MATHEMATICS, AND APPLICATIONS

ROBERT J. HERMANN, United Technologies Corporation, *Chair*
PETER M. BANKS, Environmental Research Institute of Michigan
SYLVIA T. CEYER, Massachusetts Institute of Technology
L. LOUIS HEGEDUS, W.R. Grace and Company (retired)
JOHN E. HOPCROFT, Cornell University
RHONDA J. HUGHES, Bryn Mawr College
SHIRLEY A. JACKSON, U.S. Nuclear Regulatory Commission
KENNETH I. KELLERMANN, National Radio Astronomy Observatory
KEN KENNEDY, Rice University
THOMAS A. PRINCE, California Institute of Technology
JEROME SACKS, National Institute of Statistical Sciences
L.E. SCRIVEN, University of Colorado
LEON T. SILVER, California Institute of Technology
CHARLES P. SLICHTER, University of Illinois at Urbana-Champaign
ALVIN W. TRIVELPIECE, Oak Ridge National Laboratory
SHMUEL WINOGRAD, IBM T.J. Watson Research Center
CHARLES A. ZRAKET, MITRE Corporation (retired)
NORMAN METZGER, Executive Director

THE NATIONAL ACADEMIES

National Academy of Sciences
National Academy of Engineering
Institute of Medicine
National Research Council

The **National Academy of Sciences** is a private, nonprofit, self-perpetuating society of distinguished scholars engaged in scientific and engineering research, dedicated to the furtherance of science and technology and to their use for the general welfare. Upon the authority of the charter granted to it by the Congress in 1863, the Academy has a mandate that requires it to advise the federal government on scientific and technical matters. Dr. Bruce Alberts is president of the National Academy of Sciences.

The **National Academy of Engineering** was established in 1964, under the charter of the National Academy of Sciences, as a parallel organization of outstanding engineers. It is autonomous in its administration and in the selection of its members, sharing with the National Academy of Sciences the responsibility for advising the federal government. The National Academy of Engineering also sponsors engineering programs aimed at meeting national needs, encourages education and research, and recognizes the superior achievements of engineers. Dr. Harold Liebowitz is president of the National Academy of Engineering.

The **Institute of Medicine** was established in 1970 by the National Academy of Sciences to secure the services of eminent members of appropriate professions in the examination of policy matters pertaining to the health of the public. The Institute acts under the responsibility given to the National Academy of Sciences by its congressional charter to be an adviser to the federal government and, upon its own initiative, to identify issues of medical care, research, and education. Dr. Kenneth I. Shine is president of the Institute of Medicine.

The **National Research Council** was organized by the National Academy of Sciences in 1916 to associate the broad community of science and technology with the Academy's purposes of furthering knowledge and advising the federal government. Functioning in accordance with general policies determined by the Academy, the Council has become the principal operating agency of both the National Academy of Sciences and the National Academy of Engineering in providing services to the government, the public, and the scientific and engineering communities. The Council is administered jointly by both Academies and the Institute of Medicine. Dr. Bruce Alberts and Dr. Harold Liebowitz are chairman and vice chairman, respectively, of the National Research Council.

www.national-academies.org

Preface

From August 1994 to August 1995, the National Research Council's (NRC's) Computer Science and Telecommunications Board conducted a series of three workshops on research issues in high-performance computing and communications. The goal of the series w as to bring together specialists in selected, nationally important application areas and researchers from the high-performance computing and communications (HPCC) research community to explore unmet technology needs and their implications for research. The workshops were held at the request of the Department of Defense, Defense Advanced Research Projects Agency (DARPA). They also drew on the interest and input of other agencies that are major supporters of HPCC research, in particular the National Science Foundation, the Department of Energy, and the National Aeronautics and Space Administration. The agendas and participant lists for Workshops I through III are given in Appendix A.

The applications discussed in the workshops were selected both for their importance to economic and societal goals and for the diversity of challenges they pose for computing and communications research. The first workshop was held in August 1994 at the Arnold and Mabel Beckman Center of the National Academy of Sciences and the National Academy of Engineering in Irvine, California. It considered applications in four areas of national importance: manufacturing (e.g., simulation, collaborative design) ; health care (e.g., computerized patient records, medical information, telemedicine); digital libraries (e.g., electronic storage, search and retrieval of multiple forms of information); and electronic commerce and banking (e.g., secure, distributed transactions).

Although significant insights were gained from examining this broad set of applications, the steering committee decided to explore a single application area in detail to enhance understanding of computing and communications requirements both for that area and for national applications in general. In consultation with DARPA, the steering committee selected crisis management for focused study. Crisis management incorporates preparation for, response to, and recovery from natural and technological disasters such as hurricanes, earthquakes, and oil spills; political-military crises; and related emergencies. Crisis management seemed an ideal focus because its diverse problems create demands for a number of different high-performance technologies. These range from high-performance computation to high-bandwidth, intelligent, and secure communications and information systems, as well as tools to support decision making and management of distributed groups of actors in a complex, uncertain, and rapidly changing environment (analogous to command and control in military operations). Crisis management also provides a context for evaluating both where specifically high-performance technologies can make a significant contribution and where knowledge gained from research can lead to valuable advances in more mainstream (i.e., nonhigh-performance) technologies.

The second workshop, held at the Beckman Center in June 1995, examined the problems presented by crisis management and the strengths and shortcomings of existing computing and communications technologies for addressing them. Both civil and military crisis management were considered, although civil applications received more attention. The steering committee and workshop participants found crisis management to be an especially fruitful source of research topics that have the potential to advance the state of computing and communications on a broad front, in addition to meeting some of the pressing technology needs of civilian and military crisis managers.

The final workshop, held in August 1995 at the National Academy of Sciences Building in Washington, D.C., focused on defining key research opportunities that should be pursued to meet the needs of application areas addressed in the first two workshops . That workshop continued the emphasis on crisis management but also revisited the other application areas from the first workshop as additional sources of input and as a test of the generality of conclusions about crisis management needs.

This report synthesizes and elaborates on what was learned in the three workshops. The steering committee emphasizes that it was not the goal of the series to provide recommendations on how to solve the specific problems of crisis management and other application areas in the nation today. Solving crisis management problems such as slow or incomplete delivery of food, medicine, information, and financial assistance to people affected by a disaster requires resources, expertise, and effort in many areas in addition to computing and communications (e.g., effort to address budget constraints for local and state crisis management agencies, interagency coordination, personnel training). Rather, the workshops' goal was to explore applications to gain insights into problems that computing and communications research could address, thereby helping to alleviate, with more capable or cheaper technologies, problems faced in crisis management and other nationally important application areas. In that respect the workshops proved to be a rich source of ideas for the research community to consider.

The steering committee for the Workshop Series on High Performance Computing and Communications acknowledges the contributions of the workshop speakers and participants. Their insights and creativity were central to this effort. We especially thank James Beauchamp, of the U.S. Commander in Chief, Pacific Command (CINCPAC); John Hwang, Federal Emergency Management Agency; Robert Kehlet, Defense Nuclear Agency; David Kehrlein, Office of Emergency Services, State of California; and Lois Clark McCoy, National Institute of Urban Search and Rescue, as well as other crisis management professionals who educated, stimulated, and challenged a diverse group of computing and communications researchers. In addition, workshop participants Joel Saltz, of the University of Maryland, and Clifford Lynch, of the Office of the President, University of California, made valuable written contributions to the final report.

The steering committee also thanks the NRC staff for their diligent assistance throughout the workshop series and preparation of the final report, including Marjory Blumenthal, John Godfrey, Gail Pritchard, and James Mallory. The steering committee and I are especially grateful to John Godfrey for his resourcefulness in identifying experts and information sources and his conscientious assistance in developing this report. His efforts to attract both crisis management and computing experts to join in this collaborative project and his consistent support in integrating materials and ideas from both perspectives were key to the successful outcome of this project. Gail Pritchard's assistance in ensuring the smooth running of the workshops and providing organizational support to the steering committee was also essential and much appreciated. Finally, the steering committee is grateful to the anonymous reviewers for helping to sharpen and improve the report through their comments. Responsibility for the report remains with the steering committee.

Ken Kennedy, *Chair*

Steering Committee, Workshop Series on High Performance Computing and Communications

PREFACE x

Contents

	OVERVIEW AND SUMMARY	1
1	APPLICATION NEEDS FOR COMPUTING AND COMMUNICATIONS	8
	Introduction	8
	Crisis Management	10
	Definition and Characteristics	10
	Scenarios	16
	Crisis Management Needs for Computing and Communications	16
	Other Application Domains	34
	Digital Libraries	35
	Electronic Commerce	38
	Manufacturing	42
	Health Care	47
	Notes	53
2	TECHNOLOGY: RESEARCH PROBLEMS MOTIVATED BY APPLICATION NEEDS	55
	Introduction	55
	Networking: The Need for Adaptivity	56
	Self-Organization	60
	Network Management	62
	Security	65

	Discovery of Resources	68
	Virtual Subnetworks	68
	Computation: Distributed Computing	69
	Modeling and Simulation	70
	Mobility of Computation and Data	72
	Storage Servers and Meta-Data	73
	Anomaly Detection and Inference of Missing Data	75
	Sensors and Data Collection	75
	Distributed Resource Management	77
	Software System Development	78
	Information Management: Finding and Integrating Resources	81
	Integration and Location	84
	Meta-Data and Types	88
	Production and Value	89
	Distribution and Relocation	90
	User-centered Systems: Designing Applications to Work with People	91
	Human-centered Systems and Interfaces	91
	Collaboration and Virtual Organizations	93
	Judgment Support	95
	Notes	97
3	SUMMARY AND FINDINGS: RESEARCH FOR NATIONAL-SCALE APPLICATIONS	99
	Research Challenges of Crisis Management	99
	Technology Deployment and Research Progress	107
Finding 1:	Crisis Management Testbeds	109
Finding 2:	Studies of Existing National-scale Information Infrastructure	111
	Support of Human Activities	112
Finding 3:	Usability	113
Finding 4:	Collaboration	116
	System Composability and Interoperability	117
Finding 5:	Focused Standards	118
Finding 6:	Interoperability	122
Finding 7:	Integration of Software Components	124
Finding 8:	Legacy and Longevity	126
	Adapting to Uncertainty and Change	130
Finding 9:	Adaptivity	130
Finding 10:	Reliability	134
	Performance of Distributed Systems	136
Finding 11:	Performance of Distributed Systems	136
	Notes	137

BIBLIOGRAPHY 139

APPENDIXES
A Workshop Series on High Performance Computing and 145
   Communications
B Background—HPCCI and NII 156
C Acronyms and Abbreviations 158

Overview and Summary

Crises are extreme events. They cause significant disruption and put lives and property at risk. Some crises arise from natural disasters such as earthquakes, hurricanes, fires, and floods. Man-made crises can be accidental, such as oil spills or the release of toxic substances, or they may be intentional, such as bombings by terrorists. Crises require an immediate response and a coordinated application of resources, facilities, and efforts beyond those regularly available to handle routine problems.

Crisis management was the primary application area examined in the Workshop Series on High Performance Computing and Communications conducted by the Computer Science and Telecommunications Board of the National Research Council (see Box S.1). Crisis management was selected not only because of its critical importance to public safety and well-being, but also because building good tools that are useful in meeting the extreme demands of crisis management requires significant advances across a combination of many different, broadly applicable computing and communications technologies. The challenges confronting crisis managers are extreme in several dimensions. Crises require an extraordinary quantity of resources, such as search and rescue teams, medical assistance, food, and shelter. The demands are highly diverse—implying a need for cooperation among many different actors—and largely unpredictable in terms of location, time, and specific resources needed. Moreover, the urgency associated with crises has many implications, such as the need to rapidly identify, collect, and integrate crucial information about the developing situation; to have access to tools and resources that are not cumbersome or difficult to use, particularly in stressful conditions; and to have the capability to make projections and initiate actions in the face of an inevitable degree of uncertainty and incompleteness of information.

> **BOX S.1 OVERVIEW AND CONTEXT OF THE WORKSHOP SERIES**
>
> Consultation with people who use or want to use computing and communications to accomplish their objectives provides a sometimes sobering perspective on technology design and implementation. The three Computer Science and Telecommunications Board (CSTB) workshops on high-performance computing and communications were designed to foster discussion among application specialists-including technology experts (developers or systems managers) and professionals in crisis management, digital libraries, electronic commerce, manufacturing, and health care-and researchers to explore how computing and communications technologies are used in these areas, the problems or shortcomings associated with current technologies, and potential improvements that might both enhance the technology base in these national-scale applications and advance the state of the art in computing and communications. Researchers and users discussed not only traditional high-performance concerns, such as speed and scale of computation and networking, but also capabilities in information management, collaborative work, decision making, and many other areas. Such capabilities are enabled by advances in the underlying computer and network systems and at the same time make them more useful, thus hastening the evolution of a collection of computers and communications links into an information infrastructure.
>
> The workshop series fits with the intent of several federal programs to foster greater interaction among researchers, developers, and users of leading-edge computing and communications. The framework for many of these activities has been the High Performance Computing and Communications Initiative (HPCCI; see Appendix B for a brief discussion), which has stimulated such interactions, beginning with scientific investigation of "Grand Challenges" and continuing toward study of broader "National Challenge" applications. A CSTB review concluded that the HPCCI has demonstrated the value for computing and communications

Workshop discussions covered a spectrum from research through development to deployment and use of technology. The mix of professionals fostered consideration of how the conditions in which computing and communications are used can affect the perceived value of technologies and the demand for improvement—nontechnological conditions, too, shape perceptions about the kinds of features that would be helpful. Resource constraints of local and state crisis management agencies, for example, limit the amount of training available to users of technological tools and require users to trade-off performance and other features of new technologies against the life-cycle cost of equipment.

Out of these discussions came ideas about where truly high performance technology may be helpful in different application domains, where advances in performance at the leading edge would yield benefits in more mainstream

> research of interaction between developers and users of technologies (CSTB, 1995). Related activities include a February 1994 forum involving several hundred researchers and others, "R&D for the NII: Technical Challenges," that yielded a discussion of current research topics in communications and computing infrastructure technologies (Vernon et al., 1994). The Committee on Information and Communications (CIC) of the National Science and Technology Council developed a plan for coordinating research and development (R&D) across multiple federal agencies, identifying strategic R&D focus areas that relate to agency missions and other user needs (CIC, 1995). More narrowly focused efforts have illuminated research opportunities in specific application areas, such as health care and digital libraries.[1] These recent examinations of research needs, however, have drawn mainly from the research community.
>
> By comparison, the CSTB workshop series emphasized crisis management as an application domain and featured the substantial participation of end users, including nontechnologists.[2] Traditionally, crisis management has not been a focus of academic computing and communications researchers, other than in the context of military system development. But at the CSTB workshops, crisis management inspired fresh discussion of a full range of computing and communications research issues and provided a real-world perspective for calibrating research needs related to other national-scale applications—some of which have been examined more extensively through various federal programs and private-sector activities-against one that is particularly demanding in terms of urgency and unpredictability of needed resources. Crisis management was also appropriate for framing questions relating to federal support for research in an application area that is primarily a public-sector responsibility.
>
> ---
>
> [1] For examples, see Davis et al. (1995) and Lynch and Garcia-Molina (1995).
> [2] This mix contributed to the evolution, subsequent to Workshop I, of an NSF workshop focused on health care (Davis et al., 1995). A participant identified individuals in Workshop I to invite to the NSF event, as he reported in Workshop III.

systems, and how the interaction of applications in different areas through the evolving information infrastructure, on a national scale (e.g., the use of telemedicine and digital libraries in crisis response), influences the development and use of computing and communications. This changing context highlights the need for fundamental research to understand cross-cutting problems arising in *national-scale applications* (see Box S.2) that, on a smaller scale, may appear merely to be questions of implementing known technologies. Workshop participants agreed that the formulation of research questions by researchers will benefit from an explicit recognition that the technologies arising from today's research will be deployed to meet real needs.

Chapter 1 discusses unmet demands for computing and communications technologies in crisis management and four other national-scale application areas—digital libraries, electronic commerce, manufacturing, and health care. Computing and communications technologies are increasingly central to manag ing activities in all of these areas. However, current state-of-the-art technology is not always adequate to meet existing and emerging demands. Society's dependence on information technology is not absolute; certainly, fire fighters can continue to put out fires without computerized maps, and doctors can write clinical reports with pen and paper. However, continued improvements in the quality, efficiency, accessibility, and dependability of nationally important industries and services are realizable through advances in information technology and their integration into the work practices of organizations and individuals.

BOX S.2 CHARACTERISTICS OF NATIONAL-SCALE APPLICATIONS

National-scale applications such as those discussed in this report—crisis management, digital libraries, electronic commerce, manufacturing, and health care—use computing and communications on a nationwide (even global) scale.[1] "National scale" therefore implies the potential for large volumes of computation and communications, a large number and diversity of individuals and organizations, and the associated complexity. National-scale efforts such as crisis management are distributed across multiple locations, are often linked by networks, and make use of a variety of computing and communications resources. The people involved vary in expertise, ranging from scientists and engineers to citizens who may lack specialized technological knowledge. Because they operate in such a broad and diverse environment, computing and communications systems for these application areas must be able to survive and adapt to variety and rapid change in the needs of individuals and organizations for technologies.

The national-scale applications examined in the Computer Science and Telecommunication Board's three workshops have several elements in common:

- *Scale.* National-scale applications raise qualitatively new challenges for computing and communications technologies because of the geographic distribution, extent, and diversity of requirements for processing, storage, and communication of information, as well as the number of interconnected end points-users, computers, and information sources and repositories.
- *Demand for dependability.* As people come to rely increasingly on the computing and communications systems that serve national-scale applications, these systems begin to become part of the infrastructure society counts on, as the telephone system did early in the century. Consideration must be given to systems' survivability, security, fault tolerance, and graceful degradation (as opposed to
- Consequently, whether expressed as needs of society or as opportunities for researchers, unmet demands for improved capabilities in areas of broad national significance suggest many fruitful problems for research in and development of

- catastrophic failure), among other issues. Systems must also respond to the rapid, continuing evolution of underlying technologies in a competitive marketplace.
- *Architectural diversity.* Distributed ownership of systems among many organizations and individuals makes monolithic, rigidly defined architectures largely impractical.[2] Common interests among parties in one application domain such as health care or banking may result in agreement on specific architectural elements, but these interests evolve, and so generality and flexibility are required. This requirement for generality and flexibility implies the need for common interconnection standards, as well as support for people to identify and integrate the resources available to them across multiple system architectures.
- *Heterogeneous interfaces and standards.* National-scale applications are distinguished by an enormous degree of heterogeneity and decentralization in the interfaces and models of interaction among the systems that support them. Centralized control or widespread agreement on a set of protocols and functional interfaces is difficult to achieve.[3] In designing systems to support broad national activities with many autonomous players, the determination of where, what, and how much to hold in common among system elements must be an ongoing process open to diverse—and competing—commercial implementations.[4]

---

[1] Although it is not the case that each instance of using these applications is necessarily distributed across the entire nation, one of their distinguishing characteristics is that a given use potentially may draw upon resources anywhere in the nation—in some cases, the world.

[2] Architectures are the underlying models of systems and how they relate to each other. Interfaces and standards generally embody a particular architecture; however, a standard may be used in more than one architecture, and an architecture may have more than one implementation.

[3] This is true even in a relatively centralized institutional context. For example, heterogeneity is quite evident in military systems, particularly when more than one service branch or national force is involved. In addition, because the Department of Defense and other users of large-scale systems are relying increasingly on available commercial technologies, the choice and definition of standards are becoming increasingly significant for them.

[4] The need for openness and evolution raises questions about how to achieve formal and informal standards and conventions on a national scale. The continuing need for standards to achieve interconnection and integration suggests the broad value of research that can clarify choices among alternative technologies while those technologies are being developed, can increase compatibility among technologies, or can generate new technologies that diminish the problems associated with heterogeneity.

high-performance and other computing and communications technologies. These research opportunities are discussed in detail in Chapter 2. Not all of them are new; however, from the perspective of crisis management, problems familiar from other nationally important application domains take on an added dimension because of requirements for systems and applications that are flexible across extremes of scale, diversity, and rapid change.

Chapter 3 presents the steering committee's findings based on inputs from the workshop series and a sampling of additional, related sources. Box 3.2 presents selected examples of compelling, applications-motivated computer science and engineering research topics identified in discussions between crisis management experts and technologists at the workshops. These include communications resources such as rapidly deployable, self-configuring wireless networks for coordinating response teams; "judgment support" tools to assist crisis managers in making decisions in the absence of complete, reliable information; simulations of phenomena such as hurricanes and fires that could deliver useful results to crisis managers rapidly; virtual "anchor desks" that place network-based resources such as simulations and information systems at the disposal of crisis managers; and other specific tools and technologies that appear promising for crisis management.

Finding 1 emphasizes the importance of experimental testbeds for crisis management-related research and development. Testbeds that provide a realistic application setting, such as simulation- and field-based training exercises, can serve as demanding implementation environments for new technologies and sources of feedback to identify and refine research objectives. Application users, such as federal, state, and local civilian crisis management personnel, should participate in testbed activities. Their input is essential to assess the fit among systems, tools, and users' needs and to ensure that technology is focused on usable, practical solutions.

To secure the full benefits of application-specific computing and communications technologies, there must also be recognition of the increasingly interconnected nature of national-scale applications. In application areas such as crisis management, digital libraries, electronic commerce, manufacturing, and health care, the widespread interconnection of computing and information resources and the people who use them over networks has made it feasible, and increasingly common, for resources to be called on in unforeseen ways. Crisis management, in particular, illustrates the value of being able to integrate highly diverse resources whose usefulness in an unusual situation could not have been anticipated in advance.

Unfortunately, technologies developed to meet a specific application requirement often do not function well in unforeseen circumstances because of complex, difficult problems of interoperation, performance, and scaling up. Therefore, the findings resulting from this workshop series also address research, development, and deployment efforts that can lead to both consistent architectural approaches that function on a national scale and general-purpose tools and services that facilitate rapid, ad hoc integration of systems and resources.

Finding 2 highlights the importance of investigating the features of existing national-scale infrastructures for specific applications to identify what features do and do not work. Findings 3 through 11 identify technological leverage points for computing and communications research investments, based on needs of national-scale applications. These findings emphasize research challenges in four areas: (1) support of human activities (e.g., improved ease of use of technologies for individuals and groups), (2) system composability and interoperability, (3) adapting to uncertainty and change, and (4) performance of distributed systems. Outcomes of testbed and architecture-study activities suggested in Findings 1 and 2 should inform future reexamination of these research areas, which represent the best understanding of a range of technology and application experts in 1995-1996.

The research questions discussed in this workshop report can and should motivate the scientific and engineering research communities in the future. They have the potential to increase the ability of individuals and organizations to make the most of important applications, to present intellectually stimulating challenges for researchers, and to promote significant advances in the state of technology.

REFERENCES

Committee on Information and Communications (CIC). 1995. *America in the Age of Information: Strategic Implementation Plan* . National Science and Technology Council, Washington, D.C., March 10.

Computer Science and Telecommunications Board (CSTB), National Research Council. 1995. *Evolving the High Performance Computing and Communications Initiative to Support the Nation's Information Infrastructure* . National Academy Press, Washington, D.C.

Davis, Larry S., Joel Saltz, and Jerry Feldman. 1995. "NSF Workshop on High Performance Computing and Communications and Health Care." Report of a workshop, December 8-10, 1994, Washington, D.C. Available on line at http://www.umiacs.umd.edu:80/users/lsd/papers/nsfwork.html .

Lynch, Clifford, and Hector Garcia-Molina. 1995. "Interoperability, Scaling, and the Digital Laboratories Research Agenda." Report on the Information Infrastructure Technology and Applications (IITA) Digital Libraries Workshop, Reston, Va., May 18-19. Available on line at http://www-diglib.stanford.edu/diglib/pub/reports/iita-dlw .

Vernon, Mary K., Edward D. Lazowska, and Stewart D. Personick (eds.). 1994. *R&D for the NII: Technical Challenges* . Report of a symposium, February 28 through March 1, Gaithersburg, Md. Interuniversity Communications Council (EDUCOM), Washington, D.C.

1

Application Needs for Computing and Communications

INTRODUCTION

The requirements of national-scale applications for computing and communications pose both opportunities and challenges that derive, ultimately, from the increasing capabilities of the technologies on which these applications depend. Significant increases in computation and communications performance in recent years have made qualitative differences in what can be done with information technology. For example, widespread deployment of data networks and the increasing processing and display capabilities of personal computers and workstations have made possible a powerful and highly adaptable new medium of communication, the World Wide Web. Advances in performance have raised application users' expectations about what their information technology tools can be counted on to accomplish; as Box S.2 notes, computing and communications are becoming part of the essential national infrastructure on which important sectors of the nation's economy and society depend.

This chapter identifies opportunities for taking advantage of information infrastructure to support the missions of people and organizations in five important application areas—crisis management, digital libraries, electronic commerce, manufacturing, and health care. Reflecting the language that often is used by people seeking to apply technology to solve a problem, the chapter sometimes characterizes these opportunities as "needs" for technology. Society's dependence on information technology is not absolute; certainly, fire fighters can continue to put out fires without computerized maps, and doctors can write clinical reports with pen and paper. However, continued dramatic improvements in the quality, efficiency, accessibility, and dependability of nationally important industries and services are realizable through advances in information technology and the integration of those advances into the work modes of organizations and individuals (CSTB, 1994a,b). Whether the proposed advances are expressed as needs or as opportunities, research relating to enabling technologies remains essential; it is the foundation for progress in information technology generally and for advances in the nature and uses of information infrastructure. In addition, actual growth in the use of electronic information and communications systems in the United States and worldwide creates a need for research into the complex problems of managing information and integrating information and communications services into broader human activities that involve ordinary citizens, including specialists in areas other than information technology.[1]

To explore needs and opportunities for use of computing and communications in crisis management and other selected application areas, workshop participants examined four classes of technologies, loosely reflecting a layered model of information infrastructure, with each set of technologies providing capabilities used by the higher layers. The organization of each section in this chapter reflects this classification scheme, proceeding from lower to higher layers.

- *Networking*—technologies related to networked voice, video, and data communications, including physical facilities (e.g., circuits, switches, routers), the communications services that make use of them, and the architectures, protocols, and management mechanisms that make networks function. Key aspects include, for example, bandwidth, reliability, security, quality of service, and architectural support for the integration of higher-level functions across the network.
- *Computation*—technologies related to computer processing, particularly in a distributed context. Traditional computation-intensive functions include modeling, simulation, and some aspects of visualization, among others. Key aspects include, for example, strategies for maximizing the use of processing power (such as parallelism and distribution), programming models, software system composition, and management of processing and data flows across networks, including representation of time and temporal constraints in distributed computing.
- *Information management*—technologies contributing to the creation, storage, retrieval, and sharing of information across networks. Components that may be integrated within an information management system include traditional databases, object databases for design applications, multimedia servers, digital libraries, and distributed file systems, as well as software applications that process or manage information. They also include remote sensors attached to networks. Key aspects include, for example, balance between central and distributed control, exchange of diverse types and formats of information across boundaries,

integration of real and synthetic information (e.g., in virtual environments), and easy construction of new applications from existing components.
- *User-centered systems*—technologies for maximizing the utility of computer-based systems for the people who use them, including natural human-computer interfaces, alternative modes of information representation (e.g., speech, hypertext, visualization), artificial intelligence-based decision support (including knowledge-based systems and newer techniques for coping with uncertainty), and work-group collaboration technologies. Key aspects include, for example, ease of use for individuals and groups and the ability of applications and systems to adapt to user-specific skills and needs.

The technologies for communicating and using information are highly interrelated, and this scheme is not intended to be rigid or perfectly consistent in applying a layered approach. To simplify discussion, the application area demands for computing and communications that are examined in this chapter are distributed somewhat arbitrarily among these four areas. A particular computing or communications application (e.g., tool, system) may span all of these levels—for example, an information system that helps a user answer a question. The system would assist by translating a need for information into a formal expression that automated systems can understand, identifying potential information sources (including the vast array of sources available across networks such as the Internet), formulating a search strategy, accessing multiple sources across the network, integrating the retrieved data consistent with the user's original requirement, displaying the results in a form appropriate to both the user's needs and the nature of the information, and interacting with the user to refine and repeat the search. This system would incorporate both information management and user-centered technologies, and these would rely on a supporting infrastructure of networking and computation.

CRISIS MANAGEMENT

Definition and Characteristics

Crisis management was selected as the focus for Workshops II and III in the Computer Science and Telecommunications Board's series of three workshops on high-performance computing and communications because crises place heavy demands on computing, communications, and information systems, and such systems have become crucial to providing necessary support in times of crisis. Crises are extreme events that cause significant disruption and put lives and property at risk. They require an immediate response, as well as coordinated application of resources, facilities, and efforts beyond those regularly available to handle routine problems. They can arise from many sources. Natural disasters such as major earthquakes, hurricanes, fires, and floods clearly can precipitate crises. Man-made crises can be accidental, such as oil spills or the release of toxic substances into the environment, or they may be intentional, such as bombings by terrorists. Warfare clearly presents a continuing set of crises, and although operational warfare concerns were largely outside the scope of the workshop series, many of the characteristics and computing and communications requirements of crisis management in other contexts overlap with the needs of warfare.[2] The military requirements for command, control, communications, computing, and intelligence (C^4I), for example, have much in common with the nonmilitary crisis management requirements for understanding a complex situation and preparing a coordinated response. The relatively more centralized and hierarchical structure of military command in comparison to civilian organizations, however, introduces differences in the needs for and the available approaches to computing and communications in the two contexts. As John Hwang, of the Federal Emergency Management Agency (FEMA), observed, "Military command and control is becoming a discipline; however, civil crisis management is still in its infancy as a discipline."

When does a situation become a crisis? One workshop participant observed that when he had to call up staff to run the crisis center, it was a crisis. This tautological comment underscores that the human decision to invoke extraordinary resources and management priorities implies a situation distinct from "business as usual": standard practices no longer apply. Beyond this commonsense observation, experts whose careers revolve around crisis management sometimes offer differing perspectives on crises and crisis management. To simplify the discussion and be consistent with its limited scope for investigation, the steering committee has framed these issues in somewhat general terms in examining the relationships between the crisis-related conditions in which computing and communications may be used and the features or functions of those technologies that are needed.

Crisis management has several phases or components with different time horizons. Among these are preparedness (including planning and training), crisis avoidance (averting a developing crisis), response, and recovery.[3] Much of the discussion at the workshops centered on response-related activities, which offer particularly severe challenges across a range of technologies. Response to a crisis involves an initial reaction with available resources, a rapid assessment to determine the scope of the problem, mobilization of additional resources (such as personnel, equipment, supplies, communications, and information), and integrating resources to create an organization capable of managing and sustaining the required response and recovery. During and after the response, the need to disseminate information to the public, including the press, is an important part of the context within which crisis managers operate. The workshops also addressed questions of preparedness, since preparations and plans can alleviate difficulties associated with response and recovery from a crisis.

Requirements at each phase differ. For example, conventional (e.g., scheduled) training is needed for the earlier phases, while at crisis time, "just-in-time" training is needed to bring people up to speed. Recognition of pre-crisis phases illuminates opportunities for specific preparations, such as the simulation of possible crises to identify likely needs, which can guide the pre-positioning of resources in anticipation of predictable kinds of crises (e.g., earthquakes, floods, or tornadoes in areas prone to such natural disasters) or the formation of plans to access them when needed. An analogy may be made to the emergency room of a hospital. Statistical expectations may help to pre-position equipment, supplies, and trained staff. During holidays, traffic accidents tend to increase. This situation can be handled with an increase in emergency room staffing and supplies to meet the predicted demand; however, the next emergency that is wheeled in the door is usually not predictable as to specifics. A major crisis that overwhelms the capacity of the emergency room in a way that cannot be predicted requires contingency plans and coordination with other organizations, in order to locate and bring in additional resources or to divert patients elsewhere.

These tasks grow increasingly complex at scales larger than a single emergency room, where many organizations and kinds of resources become involved. Many such tasks relate directly to or make use of computing and communications, since important resources for crisis response and recovery include information repositories, computing capacity, and emergency communications links. Two sets of broad goals for using information resources to support crisis management, one from FEMA and one from the nongovernmental National Institute for Urban Search and Rescue (NI/USR), are presented in Box 1.1.

Workshop participants identified several distinctive characteristics of crises and factors relevant to managing them:

- *Magnitude.* Crises overwhelm available resources. (This is the distinction made, at least for the purposes of the workshop series, between crises and emergencies.) In many cases, problems that are manageable at one level become crises as the magnitude of the problem increases beyond normal or expected bounds, thus overwhelming the resources on hand. An automobile accident or a fire in a single building requires emergency services—fire engines and ambulances are dispatched—but does not overwhelm those services and so is not a crisis. Overload situations may lead to crises. They may arise, for example, in telephone systems, power plants, weather centers, and hospital emergency rooms. Hospitals in a region may be prepared for a certain number of emergency patients within a 24-hour period, but will experience a crisis if ten times as many patients arrive.
- *Urgency.* Crises have a serious, immediate impact on people and property and require an immediate response. Lifesaving fire, rescue, and emergency medical services are clear examples. Citizens also want immediate access to information about obtaining disaster relief, such as emergency loans to replace lost homes and property, and rapid processing of claims. In some crises, a fast

BOX 1.1 GOALS FOR USING INFORMATION RESOURCES IN CRISIS MANAGEMENT

At Workshop II, John Hwang, of the Federal Emergency Management Agency (FEMA), identified four major areas for applying information technology:

- Situation assessment, both immediately after a crisis begins and updated throughout the crisis;
- Emergency lane communications so that emergency managers can communicate despite structural damage and traffic congestion—including broadband communications;
- Public access to emergency information, such as warnings, directions to shelters, and ways to obtain relief afterwards; and
- Claims processing after the crisis.
- The FEMA Information Systems Directorate's "Strategic Plan for Information Resources" (September 30, 1994)[1] sets the following goals:
- Reduce the effect of potential or impending disasters.
- Improve training and exercising through the use of information technology.
- Enhance the local, State, and Federal Government's ability to set up response operations and provide direct disaster assistance after a Presidential disaster declaration.
- Improve victim registration and processing.
- Increase the availability and timeliness of emergency management information.
- Better coordination of Federal, State, and local emergency management functions.

The National Institute of Urban Search and Rescue provides the following vision statement:[2]

"Vision 2000": Crisis Information System

Without such a [crisis information] system there can be no coordinated, cost effective, efficient response. We have established the following goals for the crisis communication architecture:

To Deliver the Right Information
To the Right People
Within the "Action Cycle"
To Save the Greatest Number of Lives
To Protect the Largest Amount of Property
To Contain the Event at the Lowest Possible Level
To Guarantee a Sustainable Economy for the United States.

---

[1] Available from the FEMA Information Systems Directorate home page at http://femapub1.fema.gov/fema/infosys.html.

[2] Available from NI/USR home page, http://www.silcom.com/~usar.

- response may reduce the need for later countermeasures. For example, in a communications network overload, a cascading problem may be avoided by isolating the failure quickly, thereby diminishing the need for greater corrective measures later. Although more slowly developing, broad-scale problems such as global climate change, disease, or overpopulation are crises of a long-term nature, workshop discussion generally centered on shorter-duration events with severe time pressures. (However, it is important to note that long-term effects may influence planning for short-term crises; for example, Steven Smith, of the National Center for Atmospheric Research, noted research suggesting that global warming is linked to an increase in the intensity of extreme weather-related disasters, such as floods and hurricanes.)
- *Infrequency and unpredictability.* Some high-magnitude events, such as earthquakes, are not necessarily unexpected, but they occur infrequently and their location and magnitude are unpredictable. Therefore, it is not feasible for agencies with constrained budgets to keep on hand the extraordinary resources needed to handle crises in every location where they might occur. The nature of the warning influences the ability to respond; earthquakes, for example, occur with effectively no warning, whereas approaching hurricanes can be tracked, although their exact landfall is difficult to predict more than a few hours in advance. Crisis management thus requires contingency plans for identifying needed resources—including resources that other agencies or organizations can offer—and deploying them rapidly.
- *Uncertainty and incompleteness of information and resources* (combined with a need to respond in spite of these shortfalls). Even with complete information, chaotic conditions during a crisis make the prediction of future conditions uncertain. A strategy of waiting and watching is not generally viable in a crisis, and so decision makers must be prepared to act despite these limitations and to change course as new information becomes available.
- *Special need for information and access methods.* Both prior to and during a crisis, there may be extraordinary needs for more and different sorts of information (both from the crisis scene and from remote sources of information and expertise), as well as for sharing and presentation of information to decision and judgment makers, analysts, workers in the field, and the public. These parties' needs create demands for information flows into, within, and out of the crisis area. Often, special tools and access methods are needed to consolidate information from disparate sources. For example, in the search and rescue efforts after the Oklahoma City bombing in April 1995, information was consolidated from many sources—including agencies with offices in the Alfred P. Murrah Building and nearby damaged buildings, architectural diagrams, city maps, digitized photographs of the scene, and reports from rescue workers—to map the buildings and determine the high-probability locations of missing people. This allowed the searches to focus on those locations, thereby avoiding useless and dangerous searches of lower-probability locations.

- *Multidimensionality.* Some events become crises because of their multidimensional nature and side effects. A crisis that damages the transportation system can create crises in systems that depend on transportation, such as medical services; it may also inhibit a rapid response, thus worsening the problem. A power failure in New York during a heat wave may cause not only health and safety risks for people caught in a subway system, but also economic disruption due to the interruption of computer-based financial transactions (e.g., stock trading). Several workshop participants commented on the greater consequences associated with physical events that caused economic disruption, especially disruption to the financial system of the country or world.
- *Location and social context.* Where a crisis occurs influences its nature and the ability to respond. Many communities apply a rational cost-benefit analysis that gives planning for highly unlikely events a low priority. Thus California, which expects to have earthquakes, is better prepared for them than are other states. Crises may be international, national, regional, state, or local in scope. International events have the broadest set of issues, but perhaps lower expectations from the U.S. public for speed and comprehensiveness of response.

The political and social context can create resource limitations in local crisis management. This has obvious implications for communities' preparation for crises, among which is limited ability to acquire and use information technologies effectively. As Nicole Dash, of the University of Delaware, stated,

> In addition to technological advancements, we must also look at the human elements. One of our first priorities is to recognize that emergency management is often not a high priority in many communities. Community risk assessment tends to employ a rational choice approach in an attempt to balance cost and benefit. Because disaster is seen as rare, emergency planning is associated with high cost and low benefit. . . . In addition, emergency management personnel often lack the computer skills and hardware to utilize . . . technology oriented toward crisis management needs.[4]

The crisis management budget constraints of communities are outside the sphere of computing and communications research, but their implications are not. They demonstrate the potential value of research to make technology more affordable by reducing its complete life-cycle costs—making it not only cheaper to purchase, but also easier to set up and maintain, easier to integrate into existing organizational processes, and more usable without extensive training. Remote access to network-based resources and rapid deployment to crisis locations can also reduce costs to communities by making it possible to share resources. Comments in the workshops from crisis management professionals about the impracticality of learning and using complex, feature-overloaded equipment in the time- and resource-limited context of crisis management, however, showed that to realize these cost reductions, technology development must be informed by testing, measurement, and experience gained through deployment.[5]

Scenarios

Realistic crisis scenarios provide a context for understanding and analyzing the needs of crisis managers for computing and communications capabilities. The characteristics of crises discussed in the preceding section, "Definition and Characteristics," can be used in developing typical cases to motivate and test elements of a research agenda for computing and communications. Numerous crisis scenarios exist, developed by various civilian and military organizations for training and planning purposes. Access to some scenarios is necessarily restricted, in order to avoid spreading knowledge of vulnerabilities and response plans to potential adversaries. One publicly available scenario, which was used in Workshop III to stimulate and focus discussions, is summarized in Box 1.2. The scenario illustrates some of the range of demands that crises may raise.

The steering committee also developed the fictional scenario presented in Box 1.3, describing a future crisis and some of the means by which relief officials might respond, given computing and communications capabilities beyond those currently available or tested in experimental contexts such as the Joint Warrior Interoperability Demonstrations (JWIDs) discussed in Box 1.2. These capabilities are extrapolated from current areas of research. The scenario draws on workshop discussions with both experienced crisis management officials and researchers in computing and communications. The scenario is somewhat fanciful and is not intended as a prediction of future capabilities or a recommendation for particular technical solutions. Its purpose is to illustrate specific ways in which breakthroughs and incremental advances in high-performance computing and communications could be motivated by the broad range of crisis management needs that workshop participants identified.

Crisis Management Needs for Computing and Communications

Networking and Communications

When a crisis occurs, the first order of business is to find out what happened—to perform a situation assessment. Nicole Dash observed that a situation assessment poses two requirements related to communications. First, authorities (such as emergency services managers) at the location of the crisis must be able to communicate their community's situation to the world outside the crisis area; second, rapid response teams must be able to enter the area, perform an assessment, and communicate back what they find in real time. In many crises, the normal infrastructure of telephone and data networks will not be able to support these initial communications requirements, for one or more of the following reasons: the crisis is in a location with little communications infrastructure in normal times (such as a remote location or a developing country with weak infrastructure), the crisis itself has destroyed the infrastructure (as large natural disasters often do), or people overload the public networks by trying to call in or out of the area.

The U.S. wireline telephone network is designed to maintain or restore basic voice communications in the event of emergencies, but it may not be possible to depend on complete restoration of telephone service. Walter McKnight, of the National Communications System (NCS), reported that a review by NCS found recurring communications shortfalls for national- and regional-level emergency users responding to disasters.[6] These included the following:

- Inadequate voice services;
- Congested wireline and wireless services;
- Unknown radio frequencies for various relief organizations;
- Limited access to distributed information resources;
- Limited information sharing among different functional branches ("emergency support functions," such as transportation, communications, fire fighting, health and medical, hazardous materials, and food);
- Inability to send and receive electronic mail among users and regional offices (including difficulty finding users' addresses); and
- Lack of service provisioning (rapid setup) for telecommunications equipment and facilities.

Commenting on the current state of crisis communications, John Hwang observed,

> I think one of the misconceptions is that . . . we have a very robust infrastructure already . . . that automatically, in times of crisis, is ready to deal with the emergency situation. It turns out that's just not true. . . . [I]n emergencies, there are a lot variables like mobility, survivability, breakdowns, things which just don't work the way you think [they're] supposed to work. Now, what happens is instead of depending on healing the entire infrastructure and bringing it back up again, what you have to do is find a way through it, which I always call the emergency lane problem.

To respond to concern about congestion, federal agencies and telephone companies (both long-distance and local carriers) have worked together to develop the Government Emergency Telecommunications Service (GETS; see *Government Issue*, 1995).[7] This is a program to reserve voice-grade, analog communications capacity (suitable for fax and modem as well as voice) for priority emergency users, such as federal, state, and local governments and industry personnel. Users access GETS by dialing a special 710 area code and entering a personal identification number (PIN). GETS became available in 1995 and was used in the JWID '95 exercise and in response to the Oklahoma City bombing, Louisiana floods, and (through international calling) the Kobe, Japan, earthquake.

> **BOX 1.2 JOINT WARRIOR INTEROPERABILITY DEMONSTRATION 1995 CRISIS SCENARIO**
>
> The Department of Defense (DOD) conducts annual exercises for training and planning purposes and to demonstrate interoperability of the military services' information and communications systems. They are called Joint Warrior Interoperability Demonstrations (JWIDs). They seek to test and demonstrate technologies such as distributed collaboration and the use of intelligent decision aids; improved battle space management and a common tactical picture including integrated collateral intelligence information; improved joint, combined, and non-DOD agency interoperability; expanded use of commercial satellites and new switching technology; multilevel security; knowledge-based information presentation; expanded use of modeling and simulation including enhanced operations and simulation integration; telemedicine; and improved network management and planning, among others.
>
> In the JWID exercises, scenarios are used to create a framework for evaluating the performance of systems and planners in relation to valid, simulated operational requirements. Consistent with the growing military emphasis on operations other than war, recent JWIDs have addressed crisis management applications and have involved civilian agencies along with the military. The following scenario, related to natural disasters and subsequent complications, is excerpted from the description of Phase 3 of JWID '95 (conducted in September 1995).[1]
>
> An earthquake measuring 7.6 on the Richter scale is registered by the U.S. Geological Survey as having occurred near New Madrid, Missouri. The epicenter is located at coordinates 36.5N–89.6W. The Director of the Arkansas Office of Emergency Services initiates response measures for the state. The Governor of the State of Arkansas, reacting to these actions, declares a State of Emergency and forwards request for Federal assistance. In response, elements of the Federal Response Plan [the federal coordination plan for responding to crises are activated and deployed to provide immediate response assistance and collection of data necessary to determine actual extent of damages. An initial Disaster Field Office is established at the State Emergency Operations Center to facilitate emergency response teams.

Priority reservation systems of this kind do little for crisis response in regions where telephone infrastructure is damaged and not yet restored or has never existed. For these situations, wireless alternatives include terrestrial and satellite services. However, GETS does not have a mechanism for securing priority access to cellular telephone circuits, which typically become jammed during a crisis; this reduces its utility for users who must be mobile at the scene of a crisis. NCS has experimented with crisis communications integrating voice and data service via the T-1 (1.5 megabits per second) transponder of the National Aeronautics and Space Administration's (NASA's) Advanced Communications

> Most of the state utilities and thoroughfares in the northeast quarter of the state are severely damaged or destroyed. Communications are limited to wireless in the damaged area. Loss of life and critical injuries are substantial and basic medical, shelter, power, food and water supplies are decimated. Some of the initial damages include:
>
> - Seismic oscillation disrupts military communications capabilities in a southeasterly direction.
> - A truck carrying chemical and/or biological ordnance destined for the Pine Bluff Arsenal is overturned and the payload (undetonated) is dispersed over a wide area.
> - Numerous roads, bridges and interstate highways are inaccessible to emergency vehicles.
> - Public utilities are nonexistent in the decimated area. Local telephone service is disrupted and limited.
> - The populace of the affected area is without shelter, food, water and medical supplies.
>
> The JWID '95 Phase 3 exercise linked participants distributed in Arkansas and throughout the nation using the Government Emergency Telecommunications Service (GETS), which provides crisis managers with priority voice service over facilities of the public long-distance and local telephone services (Hazard Technology, 1995a). The National Aeronautics and Space Administration (NASA) Advanced Communications Technology Satellite (ACTS) and a commercial mobile data network were used for mobile communications. As part of the exercise, a state trooper "discovered" the spilled ordnance, identified it as dangerous using a database of chemical and biological hazards previously installed on his portable computer, and reported it via wireless e-mail to the Emergency Operations Center in Conway, Arkansas. There, an atmospheric dispersion model was run to predict areas in danger and to plan an evacuation and cleanup operation. Crisis managers shared maps, situation reports, briefings, weather data, and similar information over an "emergency information network," a secure subnetwork deployed over the Internet using World Wide Web technology.
>
> ---
> [1] Scenario document available from JWID home page, http://www.pacom.mil.

Technology Satellite (ACTS). The U.S. Army set up a transportable ACTS T-1 very small aperture terminal (VSAT) in a few hours during the Haiti operations in 1994 (Dixon et al., 1995, p. 27). John Hwang explained that FEMA can deploy to a field command center a mobile (truck-mounted) satellite terminal capable of digital communications at T-1 data rates (1.5 megabits per second).[8] This is sufficient for multiple voice conversations and some data communications between a field command center and authorities outside the crisis area, but it does not solve the problem of communications among mobile workers at the crisis. There is also a drawback in terms of the delay involved in driving the van to the

BOX 1.3 CRISIS 2005 SCENARIO

The trip to the opera was the high point for the thousands of international visitors to the conference. They are streaming out of the new center, which had been built in a decaying downtown area. Here, old warehouses are mixed with the new buildings of the city's economic redevelopment zone.

Luke is on duty at the crisis center when the first images from emergency video-911 calls show the horrifying sight. Gigantic explosions rock a set of old chemical warehouses, and fires and fumes of unknown composition ring the new opera complex. The frightened audience panics and scatters into the surrounding alleys and buildings, where some become trapped. Television crews covering the opera immediately switch their cameras to this catastrophe. Within a few seconds after the initial alarms, all the digital video channels on the global information infrastructure (GII) are presenting the chaos, damage, and injuries live to a world whose virtual eyes are trained on Luke's and the other crisis officials' every action.

Luke, unlike many today, is well prepared for this event. His graduate specialty was computer-supported intuitive judgment—the science of making difficult decisions under deadline pressure with unprepared, uncertain, and incomplete information. This education has been augmented with specialized simulations in the Federal Emergency Management Agency's training facility, where various disasters and collaborative response exercises were presented using experiences and technology developed from distributed interactive simulation activities of the previous decade. Within seconds of the crisis' occurrence, the command center system suggests—and Luke and his colleagues confirm and refine—the reservation of key GII resources. These include priority communications links—so-called emergency lanes on the information highway—and a wide array of communications, computational, and information resources carried atop these lanes.

Academic supercomputers and distributed metacomputers roll out their simulations of colliding black holes and other physical phenomena. Now they stand ready to model the movement of the chemical plumes and raging fires. Specialized intelligent software agents roam the GII, and key resources are identified and activated. Some of the audio and database streams associated with the crisis are routed through translation service bureaus on the GII, so that Luke, his colleagues, and the many doctors, scientists, and decision makers from different countries who will become involved in the crisis can have information presented to them in their native tongues. Advanced distributed metacomputer support on the GII allocates and links the reserved computing resources with specialized resource centers (anchor desks) for chemical and atmospheric modeling, which apply the necessary databases and reaction simulations needed for plume prediction. The software codes were written in a highly scalable language descended from High Performance Fortran so that they run efficiently on multiple, heterogeneous hardware platforms and adapt smoothly to the scale of distributed computing resources that can be brought to bear on the crisis. Parts of the modeling code were in fact written years before but had scaled successfully as underlying hardware and communications technologies advanced in performance by orders of magnitude.

The distributed models and information systems rely on fault-tolerant high-performance networking protocols and recently developed neural network-based network management strategies to ensure that the GII's high-performance communications backbone supplies the necessary secure, low-latency bandwidth on demand. The backbone evolved from a confluence of ideas, such as the fine-grained multiplexing capabilities of asynchronous transfer mode (ATM), the need to accommodate delays in communications over global distances (imposed by the speed of light), integrated services using heterogeneous hardware and tunable requests for network resources, research on microkernel protocol composition, and functional abstraction—all areas of research in the 1980s and 1990s.

The judgment support environment that Luke and his colleagues use—which extends the rule-based decision support techniques of knowledge-based systems further into the realm of incomplete and uncertain information, unpredictable demands, and support for intuitive decision making by people—was adapted from commercial products to support military, law enforcement, and civilian crisis needs. Focused, minimally restrictive interconnection standards allow the crisis management application to incorporate components and build on top of GII services designed for larger commercial markets such as health care. The thriving middleware industry supplies the necessary integration technologies, including agents, rapidly configurable wrappers and mediators, and graphical scripting environments.

Luke benefits from a natural, intuitive user interface, which maximizes his effectiveness under stress and fatigue. This capability builds on advanced virtual reality ideas and tailors the computer interface to the problem at hand. Luke sees a three-dimensional geographic information system (GIS) when viewing the spatial confusion of the catastrophe; a virtual podium when briefing news media; a boardroom when defending his actions to angry politicians; and a summer wildflower meadow in moments of thought. Monitors record Luke's actions so that the system can learn for future events. They note an increase of errors or stress that is signaled to Luke. The information filtering, data fusion, and presentation tools also adapt to Luke's condition, reducing the number of inputs to which he must react.

Luke shares the virtual environment with others from federal, state, and local agencies and private institutions (such as hospitals and universities). These people form a virtual instant response organization customized for the situation at hand. Whether supported by supercomputer or handheld personal assistant, all interact over the GII through a common environment with a range of collaboration and productivity tools. However, the presentation of the bandwidth- and computation-intensive aspects of the environment varies—for example, from text to still images to video—depending on the available computing and communication resources. In this way the GII enables adaptive linking of "come-as-you-are" computational, communications, and personnel resources.

Jane, one of the leaders of tactical operations for the crisis, is on vacation hundreds of miles away in the northern Adirondacks, but she is able to collaborate effectively with other leaders and people at the disaster site. In the area of the catastrophe, a digital infrastructure installed at the end of the previous century is augmented by wireless connections and supplies digital video and other data from thousands of sensors to image processing and high-performance multimedia server resources on call outside the crisis area. Fortunately, basic mathematics research has developed adaptive compression algorithms, which are included in the GII protocol stack, so an order of magnitude more data can be carried over these links than would have been possible 10 years earlier. Jane observes multiple, three-dimensional perspectives of the crisis scene composed of data from hundreds crisis. Because of congestion or damage to local cellular telephone networks, local communications generally must rely on fire and police radios, which do not support data networking.

> of separate cameras, global positioning system (GPS) detectors, satellites, and other sensors, both fixed and carried by relief workers, as well as views from the news media. These data are integrated into continuously updated simulations of the vapor plume spread. They are also used to verify critical, uncertain information, such as the actual location of bridges and roads that may be misplaced on outdated or incorrect city maps.
>
> The local authorities and institutions in the area of the catastrophe had fully implemented the new meta-data standards in their public records, so that Jane is able quickly to access and integrate the necessary community databases to identify medical and other crisis-relevant resources. Jane issues an alert for hospitals who can care for the unusual chemical poisonings. Medical records are fetched from distributed databases throughout the globe so that each patient is given the appropriate care. Digitized maps of the area are superimposed on the real-time images to optimally plan search and rescue operations. Maps of specific streets and buildings from tax records and architectural plans are downloaded to portable flat-screen devices carried by rescue workers at those buildings, who modify and update the maps with information obtained firsthand. Within the security perimeter of the crisis management system, proprietary data are made available, with the crisis priority temporarily overriding normal intellectual property safeguards so that crisis managers can use the best multimedia commercial yellow pages to help their personnel in the area find key resources. Tracers and trusted information agents monitor the cryptographically marked proprietary data to ensure they do not migrate out of the virtual subnet reserved for the crisis management effort.
>
> Jane superimposes a view of the latest predicted spread of toxic plumes with a GIS representation of first-aid stations and determines that one of the stations soon must be moved. When she selects an evacuation route, the judgment support system offers up live video of potential choke points along the proposed route, and Jane notices debris blocking the way. She could open a voice link with workers on the scene to make sure they clear the road, but Jane decides that those workers' current relief activities (as displayed by the judgment support system) have higher priority and selects a different, but still adequate, evacuation route. Thus, the judgment system helps Jane and other judgment makers make the best use of available police, medical, and fire fighting personnel.
>
> By morning, the crisis is over. Authorized relatives and colleagues of injured people are able to discover and remain aware of their status on a moment-by-moment basis over the GII, including public information kiosks placed at all shelters and hospitals to which survivors have been dispersed. Information gathered during the response is integrated and maintained to enable prompt resolution and settlement of insurance claims.

An example of a crisis in which initial response teams went into the field with portable computers and satellite-capable telephones (which are limited to much lower than T-1 rates) was Hurricane Marilyn, which struck the U.S. Virgin Islands in September 1995. The U.S. Army sent a 12-person early assessment team, called an "Away Team," to St. Croix before the hurricane arrived (*Hazard Technology*, 1995c). The team carried a 27-pound kit consisting of a laptop computer with commercial crisis-oriented database software and a communications set that linked with the commercial Inmarsat satellite communications service. In the first 24 hours after the storm, theirs was the only working communications system on the island, and so all official calls passed through their link. Not enough official channels were available over this link to meet the demand, and in the future, Away Teams are slated to carry more communications sets. However, no local networking among the laptops on the scene is currently supported. This limits team members' ability to share information collaboratively.

After the initial situation assessment, a rapidly assembled response structure with many people from different agencies and organizations must have the ability to communicate to coordinate their actions. As the NI/USR's Vision 2000 statement.[9] observes, current capabilities are limited to voice telephony, which is inadequate for crisis information and computing needs; furthermore, the lack of interoperability among equipment of different organizations is a serious problem that adds cost to the overall response—all of which suggests that research investments in solving this difficult problem could have high payoffs. The NI/USR statement adds,

> An [interoperable] crisis information system is not available to the civilian side of [crisis management in] the United States today. A new system must have certain capabilities to function in the worst of circumstances. . . . The system must be interlinking, have open architecture, agreed-upon standards and consistent protocols. A lack of interoperable emergency communications is the greatest cause of the unreasonable escalation of dollar costs of disasters today. The cost of response to large scale, multiagency, multijurisdictional emergencies has soared off the top of the charts. The crisis information structure must be accessible to the scene of the need.
>
> The control structure for emergency response must function in a bottom-up manner. People bleed at the site of the disaster, not in the halls of either the State Capitol nor on the floor of Congress. However, the uniformity in communications must be implemented from a national perspective within a united framework. We have dozens of layers of overlapping technologies with overlapping and often inconsistent characteristics. Thirty or 40 years of undirected growth in emergency communications has left us with our only means of cross-communications being the telephone. Telephones alone cannot and do not provide the robust crisis information system necessary today nor for the future.

James Beauchamp, of the Commander in Chief, Pacific Command (CINCPAC; a U.S. military command organization), noted that interoperability can be an especially significant problem in overseas disaster relief missions, in which military forces, government agencies, and humanitarian relief agencies from many countries may have to interoperate with each other.[10] Moreover, solutions that are complex and difficult to implement, however technically brilliant, are of no value in the urgent context of a crisis. As Beauchamp pointed out,

> The last [communications equipment] I need in a time of crisis is something I have never worked with before. If you're going to send me something brand new, one, don't ask me to transport it for you if it's very big. And two, you had better have somebody that knows how to operate it. I haven't got time . . . in the first 24 to 48 hours to train somebody new. I'm going to go with what I know. . . . I have to integrate everything I'm doing across the wide function . . . at my CINC [theater Commander in Chief] level when I'm out with the JTF [joint task force], . . . the foreign country forces, . . . probably anywhere from 30 to 75 nongovernmental or private or volunteer organizations. None of them have the same communications gear. If they have anything, a lot of them have AM [radio]; some of them have nothing at all. All of them have a different agenda and about half of them don't trust the military at all.

Security of the network is an obvious concern in crises where there is an active adversary seeking to obstruct the response. This is clearly the case in warfare and may also apply in confronting terrorism and criminal acts. The response team must keep its plans secret from hostile parties, and it must protect its communications against denial of service. Security needs are not limited to active, hostile situations. Crisis managers may need to communicate sensitive information, such as personal medical records and national security-related satellite imagery; the threat of disclosure of such information over an insecure crisis response network could leave the owners of information unwilling to share it with crisis managers. Robert Kehlet, of the Defense Nuclear Agency, observed, "When you operate at a federal level, though, you get access to databases and information that are very sensitive in nature, and you don't want to pass that out to the world in general and make it totally and completely public accessible. You just can't. That is Privacy Act information." In practice, this restriction has prevented FEMA from sharing some types of information outside a narrow sphere; instead, FEMA must handle the data itself and share the results in sanitized form (such as map images without the underlying data). Lifting this limitation might improve the flexibility of responses, but before that could happen, security technologies (as well as information security practices and guidelines) would have to offer greater assurance than they do now.

Another emerging communications issue is the challenge associated with distributed sensor networks. The Crisis 2005 scenario (see Box 1.3) illustrates how real-time data might be applied not only in simulation but also to complement other information sources. Isolated and experimental examples discussed by workshop participants illustrate the value of fixed sensor networks for both anticipating and responding to crises, if they survive the crisis itself and can be managed and integrated effectively with other resources. Kelvin Droegemeier, of the University of Oklahoma, discussed the integration of weather sensors in

APPLICATION NEEDS FOR COMPUTING AND COMMUNICATIONS 25

Oklahoma's Mesonet and the National Oceanic and Atmospheric Administration's (NOAA) Doppler weather radars in real time with high-performance modeling and simulation for severe storm prediction. Mesonet sensor data are communicated over wireless spectrum on loan from Oklahoma law enforcement users (Oklahoma State University and University of Oklahoma, 1993). A more demanding load on networks is posed by the California Institute of Technology's (Caltech's) pilot digital seismographic data network, which uses 56-kbps (kilobits per second) frame relay services granted by Pacific Bell's California Research and Education Network to carry data in real time to earthquake-modeling computers. Caltech's Egill Hauksson noted,

> The goal of real-time earthquake monitoring is to collect data in real time from sensors in the field and to deliver near real-time information and analysis with high reliability to the users in the field. Today, continuous data collection is much more demanding of bandwidth and speed than event-driven information distribution. . . .

Hauksson added that sustained long-term maintenance of a real-time earthquake monitoring system is infeasible: past experience shows that analog networks yield unacceptably noisy data and have too limited a bandwidth, while the alternative of commercial digital network services is too expensive.[11]

Sensors that could be deployed rapidly during crisis response could provide additional inputs and perhaps increase the resolution of existing sensors' coverage. Affordable sensor systems for crisis management, however, may not be available until larger commercial markets demand their development. David Kehrlein, of the Office of Emergency Services, State of California, speaking of the need for spatial data including maps, suggested that "10 years from now, when they have . . . locators in vehicles and Chrysler and Ford and GM say, 'We want this country mapped, by golly,'. . . you will get that [mapping] done. But today, those databases don't exist at that quality level."

Sensor networks do not automatically ensure data quality. Whereas the global positioning system (GPS) provides information of known reliability, other sensor networks may decrease in quality during a crisis, in ways that make their integration with models or with other databases challenging. Egill Hauksson noted that the delivery of noise-free data to models can be crucial during a crisis because "computer algorithms and models designed to deal with noisy and unpredictable data are inherently unstable and prone to failure under high load conditions, when they are most needed. If noise-free digital data are available—as opposed to noise-contaminated analog data—the data processing can be simplified and made more reliable." His comments underscore the interdependence of computing and communications technologies.

The vision expressed by NI/USR (see Box 1.1)—of a well-integrated, interoperable communications network supporting a mix of voice, data, and video communications—is beyond the reach of current crisis management, for reasons including both technology limitations and cost. Experimental systems of high cost, unknown reliability, and doubtful ease of use are not appropriate for widespread operational deployment. However, targeted deployment and experience with real users in realistic exercises (such as JWID '95) and actual crises are crucial for testing and developing technologies and research ideas (such as those elaborated in Chapter 2) to make communications systems affordable and usable in the future.

Computation

Crisis management can benefit from computation at all levels—from the forward scene of action to strategic planning and coordination at state, regional, and national levels. Crises place demands on traditional high-performance computing applications, such as modeling and simulation. They also underscore the need for a broader notion of delivering computational performance to users who require it, wherever they are located, through a balanced, integrated collection of computers, communications, and data storage spread throughout the response organization.

Traditional high-performance computing has been applied for years to modeling phenomena that are relevant to crises, such as severe storms, earthquakes, and atmospheric dispersion of toxic substances (OSTP, 1993, 1994a; NSTC, 1995). However, high-performance modeling resources have been used primarily for scientific research, rather than real-time crisis response. Forecasting by the National Weather Service, including hurricane track predictions, appears to be among a small number of exceptions as a resource derived from high-performance computation that is operationally available for crisis response planning in real time. (Kelvin Droegemeier described a storm prediction model, discussed in Chapter 2, that has been tested experimentally for real-time applications.) The ability to rapidly requisition computers engaged in scientific research and other activities, as envisioned in the Crisis 2005 scenario, would make high-performance resources available for other case-specific applications during crises, but will require both new administrative arrangements and further advances in the flexibility, affordability, and ease of use of these resources.

Not all simulation problems require high-performance computation to yield useful results. Robert Kehlet described some ways that FEMA uses workstation-based models, integrated into a tool called the Consequences Assessment Tool, in actual operations, such as speeding up relief assistance based on earthquake model outputs. For example, after the Northridge, California, earthquake, officials approved checks to homeowners without waiting for a site inspection, if their residences were in areas that simulations identified as heavily damaged. Kehlet's examples are a proof of the concept that modeling also can have practical operational value in predicting how an impending crisis will evolve and in planning a response. Given some advance notice of the path and severity of an approaching hurricane, FEMA can simulate the likely damage to population centers, helping officials plan the assembly and deployment of relief supplies (e.g., food, shelter, and medicine) to an affected area.[12] However, the ability to generate accurate inputs to this analysis—the hurricane's path and severity—is a very difficult simulation problem in which further advances are necessary. As John Hwang observed,

> What we are not very good at is phenomenology modeling; e.g., actually modeling a hurricane. What we are good at is [estimating damage]. Given some kind of hurricane, a particular path, and the intensity, we certainly can do a lot of analyses of economic, populace, and infrastructure damage, and estimate what will happen to a particular area.

Hwang's comment is especially significant in light of the particular importance of weather-related phenomena to crisis management. Kelvin Droegemeier relayed the statistic that between 1967 and 1991, 67 percent of the world's major disasters were meteorological or hydrological in nature. Modeling many of these phenomena requires high-performance computation. NOAA's High Performance Computing and Communications Office anticipates that increases in computing power are needed to improve understanding of weather and climate effects, for example, by improving the resolution of weather models and more accurately representing key features such as weather fronts and ocean eddies (Sawyer, 1995).[13] Roger Ghanem, of the State University of New York, Buffalo, noted at Workshop II that many other natural and technological disaster phenomena will also be amenable to high-performance modeling, such as forest fire and urban fire spreading, detailed structural analysis of damaged buildings, and chemical and nuclear plant accidents.

Performance is needed not only to produce more accurate modeling results, but also to deliver them in a timely manner. As Lois Clark McCoy, of NI/USR, said, "The greatest hazard with which we deal in crisis management is *time*." James Beauchamp noted that timely results are a function of more than processor speed; fast processing is useless if it cannot be applied to current (real-time or near-real-time) data, which could be the case if large efforts at preprocessing or formatting the inputs are necessary before a system can get to work on the actual problem at hand. Timeliness also requires communications and storage to deliver the results of computations where they are needed. This is reflected in Lois Clark McCoy's call for making remote resources available:

> Systems are available today off the shelf. . . . They work on PCs [personal computers]; therefore they have limited memory and their processing time is slow. To date there has been no attempt within the emergency management domain to centralize the needed high-performance computer capability for off-site processing. The product of this off-site processing could then be suitable in near real time for downloading onto the field PCs. This seems to be the next

near-term solution to increasing the power of the present emergency management software.

David Kehrlein gave an illustration of the potentially useful combination of centralized high-performance computing and field-based PCs. Computer-aided design (CAD) software proved useful in the search and rescue operation at the Murrah Building in Oklahoma City to map the areas to be searched and to correlate estimated locations of victims (based on where their offices were located before the blast) with the actual scene. A useful application, but one that was beyond the available computational resources, would have involved transferring the CAD data into a structural model and using finite-element analysis to predict the loads on various parts of a damaged building. This would indicate where shoring was necessary to prop up damaged structures and reduce the danger to survivors and rescuers from further collapses. Remote computation is appropriate for this application because relief teams in the field have, at most, personal computers available on the scene.

Simulation can potentially be useful for testing alternative operational choices, for decision support during crises, and as an aid to planning and personnel training before crises occur. Workshop participants suggested that simulation of an ensemble of related options and their outcomes in scenarios or during actual crises could improve decision making, if the models were sufficiently realistic. Before a threatened terrorist act, for example, there may be enough time to simulate a range of tactical approaches and select the one most likely to succeed.

However, more is required than modeling of physical phenomena. Phenomena that depend fundamentally on human individual and organizational behavior are complex and difficult to model realistically, making the simulation of human judgments such as the actions of adversaries and the political consequences of decisions particularly challenging. Nevertheless, there is a need for ways to model these phenomena, because decision makers require training to develop good judgment skills. Speaking of military involvement in international disaster relief operations, James Beauchamp observed:

> All of a sudden every decision [the operational commander makes] not only has a military application to it, it has a political application. . . . You have to train a guy to do that. . . . I haven't found a good model yet to really train that guy to change his mind-set from a tactical commander today to an operational commander tomorrow. We've got to give him models that show him the value of public affairs, the value of doing news interviews, how to manage the press, how to manage information, how to deal with the customs and courtesies of another country, how to deal with coalition warfare when the day before he wasn't doing any of that.

Modeling and simulation are not the only applications requiring computation; all elements of an information infrastructure can be made more capable by increased computing power. In the information arena, applications relevant to crisis management that demand high-performance computation include data mining to detect anomalous entries (outliers) in federated databases; data fusion to integrate sensor inputs with other information sources; geographic information systems (perhaps, given sufficient computing power, with three-dimensional terrain rendering); and stereo reconstruction from multiple images and video streams.

Computation applications for information management call for a balance of performance and accessibility. David Kehrlein argued, for example, that almost any improvement in placing information technology at the front lines of a crisis, such as a PC in every relief shelter, would be a valuable improvement in the accessibility of computing resources. Even maintaining a roster of survivors at each shelter and hand-carrying data diskettes between shelters would be a first step toward improving the current situation. Informing rescue teams that someone they are seeking in a collapsed home is actually alive and well in a nearby shelter is a major benefit to the search and rescue operation. In general, information management is a crucial need that can be highly complex in crises, as discussed in the next section, and it requires access to computing power at all levels of the response effort.

Information Management

In a crisis, problems can arise from both a scarcity and an excess of information. Scarcity of information about an unfolding situation must be overcome by locating and obtaining information from many different sources. Once the response organization begins pulling in information, however, a flood of information can overwhelm decision makers. As Donald Brown, of the University of Virginia, observed, "There is too much information for human decision makers to use effectively in a crisis response situation. Computer-based data fusion systems can aid human decision making by quickly assimilating and filtering information."

Computing and communications technologies can help to identify, retrieve, filter, and integrate relevant information into a manageable, coherent picture of the crisis. Alan McLaughlin, of Lincoln Laboratory, Massachusetts Institute of Technology, noted great similarity between crisis management and military command and control, in that both require improved "situation awareness . . . and a common relevant picture of the area of engagement." Lois Clark McCoy stated:

> The essence of crisis management is an effective information handling capability. Commanders must have it; analysts must have it; tactical operators must have it. Local emergency managers now realize it is possible to obtain a rapid and clear picture of the disaster . . . yet, we still have not applied these tools and capabilities to the actual command and control of emergency response operations.

The urgency of crises forces an ad hoc response—piecing together available sources by any means available. For example, search and rescue workers in major floods and earthquakes have been guided to victims by images from news helicopters (Gillies, 1994). Urgency can lead to extraordinary efforts to bridge the gaps between data sources, such as printing maps and correlating data from different systems by hand. David Kehrlein related how, following the 1991 fires in the Oakland hills, California relief officials obtained local utility maps and overlaid them with GPS data collected from the field as a way of identifying the owners of various pieces of unrecognizably devastated ground, who could claim disaster benefits. Manually registering this information against printed maps is laborious and slow.

Data sources maintained by many different federal, state, and local agencies may be relevant in a crisis. Walter McKnight listed, for example, geographic data, demographic data, medical files, and real-time weather data. Because such data are developed in separate contexts specific to each agency, they often follow different formal and de facto standards, which makes translation and integration difficult. Those who hold data may have little incentive to make major efforts to accommodate external needs such as crisis management. Thus, efforts such as a recent initiative by the Emergency Management and Engineering Society, to develop and obtain compliance with common crisis information standards are likely to progress only slowly (Newkirk, 1994, p. 305).

Geographic information systems (GISs) provide a good example of both the opportunities and current limitations of integration across different data standards. Data fusion from multiple sources, managed and presented within a GIS, can support current assessments of situations and planning for future evolution of the crisis. For example, a GIS map with building locations (drawn from a database of residences and businesses) could be combined with sensor data on wind speed, direction, and chemical composition of a toxic vapor cloud to show where evacuation must take place. Integrating additional GIS-formatted data about the current location of emergency vehicles, shelters, and relief supplies could facilitate evacuation planning. In addition to the technical challenges posed by fusion of data from mixed sources, however, variations among different vendors' GIS standards currently impede such uses. Although existing commercial GIS standards allow for the import and export of data files in different formats, the main operational processing of geographic information occurs within proprietary internal structures (Newkirk, 1994).

In addition to integrating across different standards and types of data, computational help is necessary for abstracting, adding value, and thereby turning data into useful knowledge. This problem involves much more than just translation between data formats. Integration requires recognizing connections and patterns among completely different kinds of data, such as video images from aircraft, map coordinates of structures and roads, and spoken or written field reports from relief workers. It also requires a capability to cope with missing,

APPLICATION NEEDS FOR COMPUTING AND COMMUNICATIONS 31

inaccurate, or deliberately falsified data. Chapter 2 discusses opportunities to develop and improve what workshop participants characterized as "judgment support" capabilities—information technology tools that can support the crisis manager in making judgments in unexpected, urgent situations, in which information is uncertain and incomplete.[14]

In crises, integration and analysis must happen rapidly to be useful. As Joseph Stewart II, of MITRE Corporation, observed, information management has been addressed in the battlefield context, but to solve the problem there is a need for much better integration of computing that is specifically high performance:

> Decision makers . . . must be presented with timely intelligence . . . The chore is to turn the data into useful, corroborated, validated information that may be presented to decision makers with confidence. This accrual, sorting, corroboration, consolidation and dissemination of continuously arriving data is a major task. . . .
>
> In the military situation, data arrive by electronic means and generally in a format that is prescribed. This format contains the essential elements of friendly information in easy-to-extract form, but there is much additional information that is sent along as plain text. Some data may be missing from early reports. Some information on the same contact may be referenced to differing coordinate systems if it comes from more than one observer. Latency of the information derives from delays in the communications system, poor time coordination in the field, or the inability of an observer to transmit it until he returns to friendly territory. . . . In the civil context, sources of data are "less trusted" and more varied, and no single corps has the responsibility for ensuring that data get consolidated. Moreover data may not be released by the organization that collected them, or the release may be delayed, thereby adding to the latency problem.
>
> The application of [high-performance computing] to this problem must provide a real-time solution with an in-line system that is capable of parsing standard formatted information from a variety of sources. . . . Input data could also be weighted in this system such that data with a high degree of positional and time accuracy from systems that access GPS or a triangulation system would count more heavily than other data. . . . Computers could be assigned to process data from simultaneously arriving messages, until some time-based sorting and ordering can be done. Contacts could also be compared with databases, most of which are countable but large. Processed information must then be presented to the decision makers for fusion with other sources of data that are not automated. . . . High performance is required to allow calculations to be done in real time, so that the means of processing does not add to the latency problem for later users.

Data quality is another important issue. The quality of commercially available GIS databases poses obstacles to automated integration, because data in the GIS cannot always be trusted, but it is not apparent from the GIS which data points are likely to be out of date or otherwise incorrect. David Kehrlein related that in the response to the Northridge earthquake, the commercial GIS database that was used had a 40 percent error rate in locating and identifying hospitals, primarily because of ownership changes, telephone number changes, and so on. Usually, maps must be updated and corrected at the crisis scene against aerial photographs and field reports, to identify roads and buildings that are not found where the crisis managers' maps say they are. A national effort to improve the completeness, quality, and standardization of relevant data would be one solution to the problem, but this is unlikely to occur in response to the relatively small marketplace demand for crisis management tools.

Access to databases specific to a crisis region can also be inhibited by proprietary and security classification constraints. For example, participants from FEMA reported that during Hurricane Andrew, FEMA was unable to obtain some necessary data from Dade County until it paid the county for the data. Data and system protection mechanisms, some potentially developed for such applications as electronic commerce, could help implement more rapid transfer of authority to access data, particularly if there were a way to ensure that the data's privacy or intellectual property value could not be compromised by release outside the circle of crisis management.

If the need for specific information can be anticipated, certain problems related to location and integration of information from varied sources can be worked out in advance. John Hwang described FEMA's ongoing development of a National Emergency Management Information System, in which subject area databases related to crisis management activities (e.g., regulations and requirements for obtaining federal disaster assistance) are accessible by network to federal, state, and local authorities. Among other benefits, this approach makes resource sharing possible, thus reducing costs. It also hastens response by enabling "one-stop shopping" for key information. It is not always feasible, however, to predict the need for specific kinds of information (e.g., treatment alternatives for a mass outbreak of a rare or unknown disease). It may be equally infeasible to preassemble information concerning all possible specific instances whose general usefulness is clear. For example, rescue workers need building plans—ideally in a form that can be loaded into computer structural models. However, the need for detailed plans of the Murrah Building could not have been anticipated, and it would likely be infeasible to preassemble plans for every building in the nation that might suffer a bombing attack. Rapid response therefore calls for an ability to locate, retrieve, and integrate such information during a crisis.

User-centered Systems

A powerful message from the workshops was that crisis management systems must be usable by technical nonexperts working under extraordinary conditions; ease of use is therefore a central goal. Perhaps the most visible aspect is the interface between the user and the machine. The purpose of this interface is to enable effective human-machine communication; technological capabilities such as graphical display and speech recognition ultimately are relevant only in relation to that goal. Simplicity is not necessarily the highest virtue for such interfaces, but rather, appropriateness to the task at hand and the capabilities of each user is required. Training and familiarity with tools are crucial if they are to be useful during a crisis, as James Beauchamp's comments above illustrate. The finite resources available to crisis management organizations put a premium on reducing the amount of training time needed.[15]

The issue of usability arises not only in training for crises, but during them as well. Crises put severe stress on people, because of the extreme pressures to save lives and avert damage, as well as the fatigue that comes with overwork. David Kehrlein observed that stress can lead to a measurable decline in the cognitive capabilities of crisis managers. Considering users as part of the total system makes it clear that the ability of tools to adapt to user needs and capabilities is important to overall system performance.

The system environment should provide support for communication and collaboration between people, as well as the interactions of people and computers—in the extreme, an instant "electronic administration" to support a newly created response organization. Noting the complexity of the organizational management tasks involved, Lois Clark McCoy identified the need for ways to track and control the constantly changing information flow throughout the crisis organization as a way of reducing wasted effort and improving the organization's effectiveness. In addition, the varied backgrounds, procedures, and methods of working that different collaborating groups bring to a crisis response increase the need for clear, complete communications and information sharing; a photograph or map, for example, might convey information with a persuasiveness and clarity missing from verbal communications between people under stress who are not used to working together.

To achieve the goal of what Don Eddington, of the Naval Research and Development Laboratory, described as a consistent picture of the situation shared by everyone involved in responding to a crisis, there is a need for information sharing that involves more than just multiparty voice communications and can be done without face-to-face meetings in conference rooms. To coordinate complex response efforts involving many parties, there could be value in collaboration support systems (e.g., teleconferencing) that integrate both person-to-person communications (in multiple modes, such as text, audio, and perhaps video images) and other forms of shared data, including multimedia and sensor data, in real time. Multiple levels of computing and communications performance must be accommodated, however, because crisis management necessarily involves cooperation among people with widely varying resources. In particular, integrating workers in the field—whose upper limit of resources may be portable telephones and laptop computers—into the collaborative environment involves an ability to scale across different levels of resources and adapt to variable or unstable resources in a crisis. User-controlled adaptivity may be useful, allowing the user, for example, to select trade-offs between video image quality and frequency of image redrawing and between still and moving images; alternatively, there may be automated ways to optimize these decisions. These types of scalable collaborative applications are relevant not only in crisis management but also in other application domains, including distributed "collaboratories" for academic research and enterprise systems for business.

OTHER APPLICATION DOMAINS

Although the workshop series ultimately focused on crisis management as a tool for uncovering valuable research areas in computing and communications, the steering committee and workshop participants spent time considering other application areas. These served both as additional input from which to identify research issues and as a means of testing the generality of conclusions based on crisis management. The following sections, drawn primarily from input at the workshops, highlight similarities and differences between these domains and crisis management, including specific research opportunities that, with respect to crisis management, are discussed further in Chapter 2. All of these areas have been addressed more thoroughly in other, focused reports. They are reviewed here briefly to provide a context for—and to examine their interdependence with—crisis management. Citations are provided to more extensive treatments.

The first two areas, digital libraries and electronic commerce, represent both end-user applications in themselves (e.g., educational use of libraries, consumer banking, and retail transactions) and infrastructural services that enable specific capabilities within other application areas. For example, crisis managers could turn to digital libraries for information discovery and retrieval tools or to electronic commerce for secure authentication and payment services in order to obtain proprietary information on an expedited basis.

The other two areas, manufacturing and health care, are applications that, like crisis management, may derive significant benefit from broadly distributed computing and communications technologies. Manufacturing and health care applications (other than emergency medicine) place less emphasis on urgent, ad hoc response than does crisis management, and so integration and other technical challenges can, in principle, be addressed in a less ad hoc manner. Nevertheless, these areas face many of the same challenges as crisis management for coping with complexity and diversity, integrating information and software resources, and adapting to user capabilities and needs.

The interconnected demand for and use of resources among application areas illustrate the potential for technological advances in one application area to benefit others. They also indicate the drawbacks in terms of lost flexibility of failing to accommodate the interdependencies—for example, to accommodate demands for service and access across architectures and standards that, as noted in Box S.2, are owned and controlled by multiple parties and are inevitably diverse. Indeed, one observer characterized it as a firm requirement that research on computing and communications in each application area take into account the others, noting, "You can't address one or two of them and let the others slide."

Digital Libraries[16]

Digital libraries make more intensive demands for storage and bandwidth to manage and interchange image, audio, video, and numeric information than do activities with traditional high-performance computational requirements such as modeling and simulation. Digital libraries require substantial advances in software; information management technology and practices; and the ability to process, navigate, manage, and classify not only textual data but also multimedia, sensor feeds, and numeric data. Digital libraries also represent a primary focus of research in the scaling of very large, autonomously managed distributed systems. Central issues in the successful development of digital libraries encompass the identification, development, and adoption of appropriate standards, as well as fundamental questions about the definition of interoperability among systems and collections of information at various levels and the mechanisms that can be used to accomplish such interoperability.

Finally, it is important to recognize that digital libraries are not purely technological constructs; rather, they also encompass complex sociological, legal, and economic issues that include intellectual property rights management, public access to the scholarly and cultural record, preservation, and the characteristics of evolving systems of scholarly and mass communications in the networked information environment. The requirements for reflecting this broader context in software and network protocols are poorly understood but may generate substantial computational and infrastructure demands—for example, to examine intellectual property rights and ancillary evaluative or rating information associated with very large numbers of digital objects as part of query processing and result ranking. Design of technical approaches to support the social, legal, and economic framework of digital libraries that are sufficiently flexible to recognize and support reuse within a new framework is a challenging problem that itself has significant legal and economic dimensions. As resources that comprise digital libraries are reused in the crisis management environment, it may not be feasible, for example, to stop to negotiate a license agreement for access to a networked information resource that is needed urgently to respond to a crisis.

Networking

Digital libraries place extensive and challenging demands on infrastructure services relating to authentication, integrity, and security, including determining characteristics and rights associated with users. Needed are both a fuller implementation of current technologies, such as digital signatures and public-key infrastructure for managing cryptographic key distribution, and a consideration of tools and services in a broader context related to library use. For example, a digital library system may have to identify whether a user is a member of an organization that has some set of access rights to an information resource (analogous to the privileges discussed below in the section "Electronic Commerce"). Use of digital libraries will require both adaptivity to changing bandwidth and computational resource constraints and the ability to reserve network resources. As an international enterprise that serves a very large range of users, digital libraries must be designed to detect and adapt to the varying connectivity of individual resources accessible through networks. Digital libraries will also build on a range of other infrastructure services such as electronic payments and contracting.

The availability or reliability of resources is a less central issue for digital libraries than for crisis management. If a data source is temporarily unreachable or otherwise unavailable, the user can be told to try later; however, crisis managers must make use of the best data available at a given time. Both application domains require adapting to the capabilities of user workstations and the bandwidth that is available to these workstations. Strategies that are alternatives in the digital library environment in many cases are mandatory for crisis management. For example, a digital library system can simply rank results and at some later time present them, but crisis management applications must summarize data and provide immediate overviews.

Computation

Digital libraries require substantial computational and storage resources both in servers and in a distributed computational environment. Little is known about the precise scope of the necessary resources, and deployment and experimentation are needed (Lynch and Garcia-Molina, 1995; OSTP, 1994b). From the 1960s to the 1980s, much of the research and development in the information retrieval community was constrained by the limited computational capacity of machines available to most users, particularly the inability to perform computations on large databases in near real time. Current increases in the availability of computational power are leading to a reconsideration of much of this work and may point toward the use of algorithms that are extremely intensive in both their computational and their input-output demands as they evaluate, structure, and compare large databases that exist within the distributed environment. In many areas that are critical to digital libraries, however, such as knowledge representation and resource description, or summarization and navigation, even the basic algorithms and approaches are not yet well defined, which makes it difficult to

APPLICATION NEEDS FOR COMPUTING AND COMMUNICATIONS 37

project computational requirements. It appears likely that many breakthroughs in digital libraries will be computationally intensive—for example, distributed database searching, resource discovery, automatic classification and summarization, and graphical approaches to presenting large amounts of information that range from information visualization through virtual-reality-based modeling.

In addition, distributed queries may be computationally intensive. Digital library applications call for the aggregation of large numbers of autonomously managed resources and their presentation to the user as a coherent whole. Computation can compensate where individual resources are poorly optimized for uses that involve aggregation with other resources in ways that go far beyond their original design goals. The ability of digital libraries to reuse information resources could support crisis management applications. In crisis management, for example, information in a GIS or a digital library repository may have to be reused as the basis of a modeling or simulation activity.[17] Current digital library systems, however, tend to be designed to facilitate specific classes of use of information stored in the digital library.

Information Management

Information management is at the core of digital library applications. As in crisis management, the digital library user requires access to collections of information scattered among a range of autonomously managed repositories. This information must be processed through sophisticated user interfaces and viewing applications that may offer simulation, visualization, modeling, and related capabilities. Major advances are needed in methods for knowledge representation and interchange, database management and federation, navigation, modeling, and data-driven simulation; in effective approaches to describing large complex networked information resources; and in techniques to support networked information discovery and retrieval in extremely large-scale distributed systems. In addition to near-term operational problems, approaches are also needed to longer-term issues such as the preservation of digital information across generations of storage and processing technology (which evolves quite rapidly) and even information representation standards.

Work on information management approaches for digital libraries has to some extent proceeded on two levels simultaneously, corresponding to different models of how people use the applications. One level deals with what are philosophically extensions of existing, physical libraries. These are characterized by the assumption that a person is the direct consumer of information and is managing the navigation and retrieval processes, using methods analogous to a visit to the library. The other level assumes that the human user is more distant from the actual mechanics and management of the processes of information discovery, retrieval, evaluation, and use; this level deals with intelligent agents, knowledge representation and interchange, shared ontologies, mediators, and related technologies. Information management technologies are central to both lines of development, but the technologies and approaches differ substantially between the two lines of development.

User-centered Systems

To be effective, digital library systems must be user-centered systems. Research is necessary to better characterize the needs and requirements of different classes of (potential) users of digital library systems, and to gain insight into how to adapt systems to specific user needs and behaviors. Although much digital library research has focused on "public" digital library services, public digital libraries form one end of a continuum that also encompasses personal information spaces and work-group or organizational information spaces. Linking digital libraries to personal and work-group information management systems is a central research and design issue—for example, to develop distributed systems for collaborative data exploration. There are also major demands for training and user support, as well as effective management by librarians of information repositories.

As in crisis management, one of the key issues involves information filtering, categorization, and ranking in situations where there is likely to be too much relevant information with which the user of the system must cope. However, the range of information that must be processed in the crisis management context is likely to be more tentative and questionable, and the qualification, authentication, and filtering of information constitute a much more difficult issue. In addition, crisis management has a much more demanding real-time constraint. This largely precludes the benefits of librarians skilled in evaluating and organizing information; digital libraries can allow a great deal of human or machine preprocessing. In both digital libraries and crisis management, incoming information may sometimes be incomplete, anomalous, suspect, or even actively falsified. The real-time constraint of the crisis management application requires adapting to and compensating for these problems, whereas a digital library can simply defer the data for later human review or confirmation from supplementary input sources.

In summary, many aspects of crisis management are functionally equivalent to digital library applications, but with real-time processing constraints (to meet urgent deadlines) and a requirement to operate successfully in an environment of questionable data inputs and high penalties for failures or errors.

Electronic Commerce

Electronic commerce involves both retail and wholesale commercial transactions—purchase of goods and services—across networks. These range, for example, from consumer on-line banking services to procurement of parts by manufacturers through electronic data interchange (EDI). Electronic commerce involves the use of processing and storage resources in multiple locations (both fixed and mobile), owned and managed by a variety of end users, suppliers of goods and services, and go-betweens. Because it comprises fundamental economic activities, electronic commerce cuts across—and is part of the infrastructure for—other application domains. Thus, electronic commerce can enable the procurement of medical supplies or reimbursement by third-party payers in health care, as well as the acquisition of new holdings and transfer of royalties in digital libraries, or the procurement of relief supplies and the filing and processing of insurance claims in crisis management. These examples are more a promise than a reality today, although the number of relevant pilot and actual (if small-scale) programs is growing. Limitations of current electronic commerce implementations include the inability to automate entire transaction processes[18] and restrictions of users' choice among payment mechanisms.[19] Nevertheless, simply listing the future possibilities illustrates the interrelatedness of national-scale applications and the potential for technical advances in one area to confer broad benefit. Moreover, the effective applicability or extension of electronic commerce to embrace virtually every person and organization that participates in the economy underscores the importance of technology (and standards) to ensure the interoperability of different commercial solutions without stifling technical and service innovation.

Both the nature of economic commerce, which fundamentally revolves around financial transactions, and its interconnection with other activities make security a paramount concern. Motivations include protection of personal privacy (e.g., personal spending records, health status, preferences), protection against theft and fraud (against individuals and businesses), and protection of the integrity of the systems and of the organizations that use them. Privacy relates not only to unauthorized access to specific items of data, but also to aggregation of separate pieces of information (greatly facilitated by their placement on networks) to yield a sensitive result, such as a marketer's profile of an individual's overall buying habits. The greater exposure of institutions to financial risks will change the business model, which is currently oriented to managing as opposed to eradicating risk.

The importance of system integrity is increasingly seen as national or international in scope: the dependence of financial markets on network-based systems and the network-based interdependence of businesses, industries, and sectors lead many to link economic and national security. For example, a denial-of-service attack on a hypothetical Internet-based gateway handling a large share of U.S. retail credit card transactions would create a crisis; without substantial improvements in the security of gateways, such an attack would be much easier to arrange on the Internet than on the current telephone-based system.

Computing and communications technologies are relevant to both vulnerabilities and countermeasure mechanisms; electronic commerce motivates considerable activity in the development and application of security mechanisms, concepts for security architecture, and implementation infrastructure (e.g., infrastructure needed to support public-key encryption). For example, commercial transactions require authentication and authorization of users and protection against repudiation of commitments by both buyer and seller. Mechanisms include identification technologies (from passwords to biometrics), digital signatures, and audit trails. Current public-key infrastructure development efforts focus on linking cryptographic keys with specific user identity; a more robust infrastructure would incorporate the notion of a user's privileges, which depend on potentially changeable characteristics such as credit card membership, rank within a company or organization, membership in a frequent-flyer program, U.S. citizenship, and others. This capability is also relevant to crisis management, in which privileges such as authority to access sensitive data may have to be rapidly but securely conferred on specific relief officials.

Construction of large commercial software systems, such as those used by banks (and in other domains, for example, manufacturing), continues to face the very difficult, decades-old problem of inefficiency in the programming process. Workshop participants identified the need to overcome this "programming bottleneck" as an area for continued research, through approaches such as hardware platform-independent programming as a source of potential advance.

Networking

Bandwidth and architecture are key issues for networking in electronic commerce. Bandwidth currently constrains the introduction of new services. For example, bandwidth for two-way video links between tellers and customers through automated teller machines (ATMs) could allow banks to improve service while reducing the number of bank branches. Increasing the bandwidth to tetherless systems is important if services that rely on graphics like those available through the World Wide Web are to be ubiquitous.[20] As these examples suggest, there is a trade-off between using information retrieval mechanisms that scale the types of information presented to fit the available bandwidth and increasing the available bandwidth to achieve a higher level of service for tetherless and other intrinsically limited-bandwidth access mechanisms. Of course, some transactions, such as account-balance inquiries, require only small amounts of bandwidth, but the concept of "anytime, anywhere" banking and commerce implies a suitably provisioned, broadly deployed fixed infrastructure and support for tetherless access.[21]

There are two architectural challenges for networks in electronic commerce: accommodating heterogeneity in the commercial environment, which implies a general and flexible architecture, and achieving security in the fullest sense, which includes ensuring reliable and convenient service in the face of unpredictable conditions (e.g., user errors, malicious attacks, mergers and acquisitions that change entities and their relationships). Although electronic commerce does not face the extremes of demands on and availability of resources that characterize crisis management, the dynamism and ubiquitous scope of the commercial market nevertheless call for adaptive, self-healing networks. These are particularly important in light of the threat of economically motivated attacks on commercial networks to steal services or assets (such as intellectual property, personal information, and electronic funds) or to deny service for malicious ends.

Computation

The computation required to support electronic commerce is a function of the kind of transaction and business process being supported—or the aggregate of many kinds. Broad experimentation has already begun for purposes of testing the relative merits of micropayment, aggregation of transactions, service subscription, and other models for electronic commerce. Daniel Schutzer, of Citibank, observed that computational performance in distributed systems (including communications and storage as well as processing cycles) currently constrains the ability to perform commercial transactions at very low cost, which is necessary if a market for microtransactions (goods and services purchased for cents or fractions of cents) is to emerge.

Within the confines of a single institution such as a bank, traditional, highly computation-intensive tasks such as transaction processing and fraud detection (through identifying purchasing anomalies) benefit from continued improvements in distributed computing. Added support is implied by emerging requirements, such as real-time pattern and anomaly detection for deterring fraud: a key challenge is obtaining useful results despite dealing with massive amounts of data from unknown sources and of unknown reliability. The widespread experimentation with software agents, such as brokers that search and evaluate over a wide range of suppliers, is beginning to raise questions about qualitative changes to existing computing system architectures. Brokers imply a cross-service lookup problem emerging in other domains as well, and this is a special emphasis in digital library research. Network-distributed catalogs, directories, and independent appraisal services (such as those of Consumers Union) could also aid resource discovery, as could scalable, network-wide advertising mechanisms.

Workshop participants also noted that simulation and modeling of firm and user behavior in large-scale commercial systems, such as banking and retail, may help smooth the deployment of electronic commerce applications, to the extent that important aspects of integrating technology into organizations can be simulated and tested prior to full-scale deployment. This demand—and the difficulty of fulfilling it—is similar to the call, noted above, for more realistic modeling of human and organizational behavior in crisis management training and operational exercises.

Information Management

For end users to benefit from many electronic commerce services, they will need to be able to locate and find out about them. This requires improved information search and retrieval mechanisms that are usable across differing kinds and capabilities of equipment. As in other application areas, this implies addressing complex challenges in management of distributed information resources, including distributed file and program synchronization and replication, and tools such as Web servers and Web searchers.

The extreme heterogeneity of electronic commerce implies a great concern for data standards that support information management tools and facilitate interfaces among planning and design, provisioning, production, and business systems (e.g., inventory, ordering, billing, fulfillment, and customer support). Support for multiple media, including images, sound, video, and hypertext, implies the need for continued development not only of standards for interpreting graphical and nongraphical data formats, but also of mechanisms for adapting to different quality demands (e.g., image compression) and access capabilities (end-user access and storage devices and communications links).

Because it is unrealistic to expect that all users would shift to any single set of standards, whether a current or a new one, a major challenge in electronic commerce is incorporating legacy systems, such as databases and communications systems in differing or outmoded formats.

User-centered Systems

The development of easy-to-use tools and other methods for locating information and other resources, conducting transactions, and implementing security, among other needs, is as significant for electronic commerce as for crisis management and other domains because of the expectation of involving people without significant technical training. The history of automation in retail banking (e.g., ATMs) attests to the recognition that consumers often need to be convinced that a new system is an improvement, and convenience or transparency of user interfaces and processes is a major part of that process. The growing need for system security is the area in which this practical reality is most likely to be challenged: achieving better authentication of users will place a premium on methods that both are effective and do not overly inconvenience customers (suggesting possibly greater interest in physical tokens and biometrics as opposed to personal identification numbers).

Manufacturing

Computing and communications are enabling significant changes in manufacturing. These relate to a very broad range of capabilities and functions, from initial design to delivery of products. Many aspects are captured in the concept of highly collaborative design and manufacturing by distributed "virtual corporations." Such enterprises use information technology to enable them to design and manufacture products in rapid response to customer demand. Discussions in the workshop series addressed mainly this aspect of manufacturing. Among the technological requirements that this perspective illuminates are networked computing and information resources to support collaborative design; virtual reality "test drives" that allow customer input to the design process beginning early in product development, when changes are easier and less costly to implement; and simulating the entire manufacturing process so designs can be optimized to make products that are higher in quality and faster and less costly to produce. (It should be recognized that although this view of integrated design and manufacturing presents a fairly broad perspective on manufacturing applications, there are many other issues that are more closely oriented toward production per se, such as robotic monitoring and control of assembly lines, plant capacity management, inventory management, and automated inspection for quality control, among others.[22]

Manufacturing begins with design; high performance in computation, storage, and networking is important to support rapid design, as well as redesign and customization based on past designs. In the past, much effort in manufacturing complex systems such as automobiles and aircraft has been spent on improving performance parameters (e.g., speed, range, altitude, size). These are still recognized as critical under extreme conditions, but more generally they form a design framework that is a minimum requirement. Today the key design criterion for manufacturing is competitiveness, including time to market and total affordability (CSTB, 1995b). Thus, design is far from the entire story; concurrent engineering involves a whole corporate information infrastructure, integrating the different component disciplines such as design, manufacturing, and product life-cycle support. Each of these presents its own challenges; manufacturing process optimization, for example, requires complex, multidimensional modeling and analysis. Simulation of manufacturing and assembly layout, logistics (material in, finished goods out), production flow, and material and process variability are additional computation- and data-intensive activities.

It is worth noting that less than 5 percent of the initial development costs of the Boeing 777 aircraft were incurred in computational fluid dynamics (CFD) airflow simulations—a classic Grand Challenge in this field (see Appendix B); more than 50 percent of these development costs could be attributed to overall systems issues. Thus, from the perspective of improving manufacturing efficiency, it is useful but not sufficient to advance the Grand Challenge application of high-performance computing for large-scale CFD. If only 5 percent of a problem is addressed with high-performance computing, one can at best influence fundamental goals such as affordability and time to market by this small amount.[23] Computing must be fully integrated into the entire engineering enterprise to be effective. However, the difficulty of integrating across these engineering functions is far from trivial. As David Jack, of the Boeing Company, said,

> Rationally we should be designing [a Boeing plane] from the tools [already installed] to reduce the manufacturing costs. We have some codes which we use for simulating the tooling. They tend to be rule-based. I haven't seen any clever way of handling those rules where the same rule may be used in configuring the airplane as is used in building the airplane. And you have got that huge logistical gap between the two. If you change one rule, does it change the other one? How do you manage that information? That's a problem that we're only starting to scratch up against.

Simulation for prototyping purposes could yield more useful results if integrated with both virtual and actual tools that are to be used in production. Randy Katz, then of the Defense Advanced Research Projects Agency, discussed computational prototyping as

> . . . the ultimate dream of hyper-simulation that has been with the computer-aided design community for the last 40 years: the idea that you could have specialized accelerator hardware that could run simulations for you, [located] at special places across the network. You might include in your simulation actual processing equipment (e.g., ovens, furnaces and photolithography equipment); they will be connected, have a network interface on them. You'll like to be able to understand whether you can build a particular semiconductor process from end to end where some of the equipment exists, some is being designed, the process itself is being designed, combining a capability for simulation with the actual use of hardware devices that may exist.
>
> There are a lot of discovery, linkage, conversion, authentication, payment kinds of issues that take place in this kind of environment. You have to find the service providers . . . [and] be able to have assurances about intellectual property rights, just as you would with anything else you might decide to publish which could be copied and handed out without your knowledge. And, of course, you would like the use of these specialized pieces of equipment to be fee-for-service.

Although the design phase is not itself a major cost item, decisions made at this stage lock in most of the full life-cycle cost of an aircraft, with perhaps 80 percent of total cost split roughly equally between maintenance and manufacturing. Thus, computational analysis should be applied in the design phase not only to optimize the product's performance parameters, but also to shorten the design and development cycle itself (reducing time to market) and to lower the later ongoing costs of manufacturing and maintenance.

A hypothetical scenario from aircraft design illustrates how the integrated, design-for-manufacturability approach to engineering demands advances in computing and communications. The example considers design of a future military aircraft, perhaps 10 years in the future. This analysis is taken from a set of NASA-sponsored activities centered on a study of the Affordable Systems

Optimization Process (ASOP), which involved an industrial team including Rockwell International, Northrop Grumman, McDonnell Douglas, General Electric, and General Motors.[24] ASOP is one of several possible approaches to multidisciplinary analysis and design (MAD) and the results of the study should be generally valid for these other approaches. ASOP is designed as a software backplane (distributed across the nation) linking eight major services or modules. These are the design (process controller) engine; visualization toolkit; optimization engine; simulation engine; process (manufacturing, producibility, supportability) modeling toolkit; costing toolkit; analytic modeling toolkit; and geometry toolkit. These are linked to a set of databases defining both the product and the component properties. The hypothetical aircraft design and construction project could involve 6 major companies and 20,000 smaller subcontractors. This impressive virtual corporation would be very geographically dispersed on both a national and, probably, an international scale. The project could involve some 50 engineers at the first conceptual design phase. The later preliminary and detailed design stages could involve 200 and 2,000 engineers, respectively.

The design would be fully electronic and would demand major computing, information systems, and networking resources. For example, some 10,000 separate programs would be involved in the design. These would range from a parallel CFD airflow simulation around the plane to an expert system to plan location of an inspection port to optimize maintainability. There are a correspondingly wide range of computing platforms from personal computers to high-performance platforms and a range of languages from spreadsheets to High Performance Fortran. The integrated multidisciplinary optimization does not involve linking all these programs together blindly, but rather a large number of sub-optimizations involving a small cluster of base programs at any one time. However, these clusters could well require linking geographically separated computing and information systems.

Because an aircraft is a system that must function with very high reliability, a strict coordination and control of the many different components of the aircraft design is needed. In the ASOP model, there will be a master systems database with which all activities are synchronized at regular intervals, perhaps every month. The clustered suboptimizations represent a set of limited excursions from this base design, which are managed in a loosely synchronous fashion on a monthly basis. The configuration management and database system are both critical and represent a major difference between manufacturing and crisis management, where in the latter case, a real-time "as good as you can do" response is more important than a set of precisely controlled activities.

Networking

Intra- and interfirm collaboration among engineers and linked simulations and databases requires reliable, secure, and interoperable communications. The need for simulations to exchange large proprietary datasets leads to major requirements on both security and bandwidth for the communications infrastructure. Integrating actual tools together with virtual ones poses a specific research challenge for new control protocols that behave in predictable, understood ways across the actual-virtual boundary. More generally, information infrastructure supporting communication both between collaborating firms and within firms (e.g., manufacturing process control) is crucial to enabling the agile, distributed style of manufacturing envisioned in this section.

Computation

The computing resource for multidimensional optimization reflected in the ASOP scenario requires linkage of a wide variety of distributed machines ranging from small to large systems. This area is a severe test for metacomputing systems that support the synchronization and linkage of heterogeneous computing devices. These distributed simulations must be linked to the many databases involved in design and to the engineers making design decisions. Availability and performance requirements of distributed resources are likely much more predictable and stable than in the crisis management context; nevertheless, ease of setting up operational systems across organizational boundaries is a challenge to the success of distributed, collaborative projects.

Information Management

In manufacturing, there is a very structured set of databases that needs to be reliably interfaced with work flow, configuration management, and other tools. Crisis management, by contrast, emphasizes good interfaces to unanticipated databases. Manufacturing databases need to have high-performance capabilities when used to drive or support simulations. Critical to the successful linkage of many corporations with (logically if not physically) central information systems is the use of standards both in system (software) interfaces and in product data definitions. In the latter case, there could be some useful interactions between information technology standards development activities, such as Virtual Reality Modeling Language (VRML) for three-dimensional object representation, and industrial production standards development such as PDES/STEP (Product Data Exchange using the Standard for the Exchange of Product model data; CSTB, 1995b).

Another critical problem in ASOP is integrating legacy systems. It is not economically reasonable to assume that industry will rewrite from scratch the large number of existing programs (10,000 in the scenario above), nor will firms rebuild all their databases to new information infrastructure standards. Using these resources across a broadly deployed information infrastructure requires advances in general-purpose, easily configurable technology for software

APPLICATION NEEDS FOR COMPUTING AND COMMUNICATIONS   47

integration (discussed in Chapter 2), for example, to take existing codes in multiple languages (e.g., Fortran, C, Lisp, Excel) and integrate them into a single, distributed system.

User-centered Systems

Both in crisis management and in manufacturing, critical decisions are made from composite systems involving humans, computers, and information systems. In crisis management, the emphasis is on intuitive judgment making with incomplete information. Manufacturing also requires good judgment for decision makers, but it represents a more classic decision support context that supplies engineers with information targeted very precisely at well-defined questions. These decisions need to be made by collaborations of geographically distributed engineers. This implies a need for collaboratory systems that link people and the information they need to make decisions.

Health Care[25]

Computing and communications increasingly affect health care in many different forms. Among those discussed in the workshop series were direct patient care, medical research, development of new medical technologies, and management of financial and other aspects of health services. Health care will continue to be administered by a diverse collection of providers working in a very large number of geographical settings. The health care system in the future likely will be characterized by (1) integration of widespread databases; (2) digitization of most health care data modalities (e.g., x-rays, magnetic resonance imaging (MRI)), allowing their transmission across networks; and (3) increased application of telemedicine. Health care providers will need to discover and access information from many sites in order to be able to put together a comprehensive description of a patient's medical history. Although perhaps to a lesser extent than in crisis management, there are significant variability and unpredictability in both the types of information that must be obtained (text records, handwritten notes, medical imagery) and their location. For example, an integrated health care information infrastructure will be able to give providers ready access to an accurate and detailed account of a patient's medical history. Networked access could compensate for the current, almost complete lack of access to patient medical records in some kinds of crises, such as large natural disasters. At the same time, however, the infrastructure must protect the security and confidentiality of personal information.

Medical decision support systems are increasingly used to help providers identify and evaluate different diagnostic workups and treatment plans. The ability to easily obtain large sets of longitudinal patient records will greatly facilitate the ability to carry out meaningful comparative analysis for clinical care and for health science and clinical research. Medical researchers and health care system administrators need to link multiple patient databases to one another and to auxiliary databases used to define such items as hospital facilities and procedures. Data must be encoded in a reasonably uniform fashion using standard vocabularies being developed—in the face of great challenges in achieving consensus among diverse parties—by the health care industry and medical informatics communities with the National Library of Medicine. Delays in formulating and agreeing on these standard vocabularies are part of the implementation context for health care computing and communications, and they are indicative of the challenge of hammering out a consensus on standards in most national-scale application areas.

Networking

The health care-specific applications of networking revolve around telemedicine. Telemedicine will enable remote consultation with individuals in their homes (an advantage for both mobility-impaired and rural patients) and with remote specialists. Telemedicine should support not only voice and video communications, but also real-time data from a range of medical sensors such as heart monitors and blood chemistry analyzers. Although the bandwidth requirements associated with textual medical record information are modest, digitization of most health care modalities will lead to increasing bandwidth requirements. The need to deliver the data to remote computing resources for processing and integrating in real time also adds complexity to the management of the overall application—for example, integrating, on one hand, the requirements of voice communications for low latency even at the expense of reduced quality with, on the other hand, sensor data that may require low-noise characteristics to be useful. Integrating real-time sensor data—including data from field-deployed sensors, as in telemedicine—into a continuously updated patient record is another potentially valuable application.

In addition to bandwidth and service requirements, difficult security issues arise because of the confidential nature of health care records and the potentially large number of health care providers who have a need to know about particular aspects of a patient's medical record. Strong guarantees of privacy, protection, and authentication will be required.[26] New models of privacy and protection are needed to address emergency "need-to-know" circumstances, while providing for secure protection of privacy. The type of de facto protection afforded by the current health care system, which still is based largely on paper and disconnected computer systems, will diminish as medical information is placed on networks and powerful information location and retrieval mechanisms become available.

There are important similarities between the requirements associated with emergency health care and crisis management. Network management must cope with near-real-time constraints that arise in emergency situations. Priority

APPLICATION NEEDS FOR COMPUTING AND COMMUNICATIONS 49

schemes must be structured to give priority to queries related to caring for emergency and critical care patients. During applications that are critical to life (such as image processing or expert assistance during surgery), uninterrupted, reliable service is vital. If the computational and network resources used for these applications are being used at the same time for other applications, mechanisms must be in place to prevent the denial of service due to resource limits.

Computation

The ability to generate large databases of longitudinal clinical records, combined with substantial computational resources, will enable statistically meaningful comparative analysis for clinical care and health science research. This analysis could enable identification of medically distinct models and templates to describe diagnostic workups and care plans, thereby improving the efficiency and effectiveness of health care. Secure methods are required, however, to disaggregate the information needed for such analysis from data that could be used to identify individuals.

Routine testing is another potentially important computational demand. There are a number of high-volume, computationally intensive image screening applications (such as mammograms and Pap smears) in which semiautomated, well-implemented image processing methods could have a strong positive impact on efficiency and accuracy. Although real-time processing is not critical in this area, the huge volume of data to be processed imposes serious requirements for computational power. In addition, whereas some routine testing examples would simply involve the analysis of individual acquisitions, more robust methods would also include database acquisition and manipulation. One potentially valuable example is the use of change detection algorithms in mammography, in which a current scan is normalized and registered to a previously acquired scan of the patient; then the two are compared to highlight potential differences. Such an application would be enhanced further by the ability to register a new scan automatically to a canonical (standard healthy) reference or atlas, including estimating the deformation of the scan to account for patient variability. By registering to an atlas, any detected anatomical changes could be interpreted further based on knowledge of the tissue type associated with the matched portion of the atlas. Image processing is of course just one of many potential data inputs about patients that could benefit from this type of semiautomation. Computer-based patient status tracking, automatic record updating, and detection of changes and anomalies could be applied across a wide range of medical sensor inputs as well as clinical observations by health practitioners.

Significant computational challenges arise in the context of areas associated with integrating robotics and image processing. The medical community increasingly seeks minimally invasive surgical procedures, with the expected benefits of reduced complications, reduced trauma for the patients, and reduced length of hospital stays, leading to reduced costs and an increased quality of life for patients. More effective use of minimally invasive procedures requires improvements in automatic or semiautomatic methods to localize anatomical structures for the surgeon and to facilitate presurgical planning. These methods should also support navigation of devices (by robot or surgeon) within the body and delivery of treatment and procedures in minimally invasive ways.

One example of a significant computational challenge is enhanced reality visualizations, in which segmented and labeled anatomical models, acquired through three-dimensional medical sensors (such as MRI and computerized tomography (CT)) are automatically registered with the patient and displayed to the surgeon in a superimposed visualization showing internal structures directly overlaid on top of the patient, from the correct viewpoint. Ideally, such structures would be tracked and their registration refined over time, to maintain a consistent visualization as the surgeon changes view, the patient moves, and the patient's tissues deform. This problem is particularly relevant in endoscopic applications, where the surgeon has a limited field of view and navigation and localization become critically important.

A second challenge is the use of robotic devices to assist a surgeon.[27] Such devices include remote manipulation and tactile feedback devices for palpation of internal tissue, systems to deliver surgical tools and procedures to inaccessible locations (e.g., in sinus surgery), and tools to improve the accuracy and reliability of surgical procedures. Key computing requirements in these applications are real-time processing, high-bandwidth data storage and retrieval, and computational and data reliability.

The creation of new medical devices can benefit from more extensive use of computer simulation. Simulations can reduce the time required to complete a design as well as the time needed for testing. With good three-dimensional models, the designer can evaluate the effect of various device parameters in its future physiological environment. For example, the ability to perform accurate simulations of blood flow through the heart with an artificial valve would help in the design of such devices. High-performance computing could allow the implementation of a more accurate model of the heart and greatly reduce the time it takes to perform such a complex simulation. Computational chemistry and molecular modeling are being applied to drug design, with scope for continued improvement as greater computing resources become available.

There are potentially important overlaps between the types of computations that need to be carried out in the contexts of health care and crisis management. Both application areas make significant use of sensor data, and both will potentially benefit from different forms of data fusion. Both areas can benefit from increased use of simulation. Because medical care is an important facet of crisis management, the ability to access patient records would also be of potential use to crisis managers in providing postdisaster medical care. If crisis managers have information about the individuals affected by a disaster, an ability to access their longitudinal medical records could be used to help prioritize relief efforts by determining which individuals might have preexisting conditions requiring special attention.

Information Management

To coordinate patient care, it is necessary to be able to integrate inputs reliably from a subset of a very large number of heterogeneous databases. It should be possible to construct longitudinal medical records recording the care and health of each individual, by discovering and integrating distributed information obtained from multiple health care providers. Resource discovery is an important need because, in many cases, neither patients or providers are able to recall or locate key past health care providers. There is also a need to locate representative case histories for comparative purposes. Although some of these tasks can be performed in advance of emergencies, this is not always possible. In addition, integrating medical sensor data to update patient status adds further complexity and real-time constraints. The real-time character of medical emergencies (particularly if they occur in the large-scale context of a disaster or other crisis) highlights the importance of efficiency of these resource discovery and retrieval mechanisms.

Currently only a small fraction of electronically stored medical data is in a form that is readily usable in automated clinical analyses, such as studies of treatment effectiveness. This situation will change as current practice improves and the health care community moves from computer databases that are largely oriented toward billing to databases aimed at recording information relevant to observing and improving individuals' care and health. The ability to obtain and process large sets of longitudinal patient records would greatly facilitate the ability to carry out meaningful comparative analysis both for clinical care and for health science and clinical research. There is a range of architectural approaches available for aggregating data for use in health systems research and in epidemiological studies. At one extreme is World Wide Web technology with knowledge agents accessing the database, which itself is in distributed form. The other extreme involves the occasional collection of needed information to a central aggregated database, which is then mined. (A centralized database incorporating medical records of everyone in the United States would be infeasible with current technology,[28] and so this should be understood as an extreme example, beyond current capabilities.) Intermediate solutions correspond to generalizations of data-caching strategies familiar in parallel and distributed computing (e.g., dividing the data and storing each part closest to where it will be needed for access or processing).

Aggregating patient records for health research raises problems of maintaining the privacy of personal information, because it is difficult to sanitize patient records by removing all data that could disclose a patient's identity (including telephone numbers, addresses, birthdates, and others). These problems are made more complex if the later identification of individuals by aggregating these data with other information sources such as financial records is also to be deterred. These threats indicate opportunities for technological advances to help prevent such compromises of privacy while facilitating legitimate research (IOM, 1994).

Both health care and crisis management share a need to search a heterogeneous collection of databases. In the health care context, it usually is not necessary to access databases that have unanticipated qualitative features. Both emergency health care and crisis management share analogous security and policy issues associated with the need to access crucial information rapidly without incurring significant security-related delays.

User-centered Systems

An integrated health care information infrastructure would be capable of giving providers ready access to an accurate and detailed account of a patient's medical history. However, this information is useful only if the caregiver can readily obtain and understand critical information, especially during emergencies. Significant, continued research efforts are needed to improve both the caregiver's ease of using medical information systems and the ease with which caregivers may insert new clinical information electronically into patient records. These embody issues both within and outside computing and communications technology. Examples of the former include user interfaces, natural language processing, and handwriting recognition, whereas broader implementation contexts might include incorporating informatics into medical school curricula.

Even with access to all available information, health care providers are often faced with—and are trained for—making intuitive decisions when available information is not complete. Economic pressures in the health care industry, however, have created a need for providers to justify the medical treatment they provide. This pressure is spurring research into the development of health care decision support. One important area that may underlie the development of decision support systems is the need for standard encoding processes to represent care plans and diseases. (This is not only a problem of finding technically optimal encoding schemes; as noted above, there are also challenges in reaching consensus among diverse parties about what names to use to distinguish various diseases, conditions, treatments, and the like.) These techniques should support the development of process representations, the automatic detection of processes from database records, and identification of similar process representations. This is analogous to crisis managers' need for support in making judgments, but with less unpredictability about the types of decisions that must be made, and therefore the ability to tailor rule-based decision support systems toward specific questions.

Health care would also benefit from increased deployment of remote collaboration technologies optimized for telemedicine, teleradiology, and perhaps telesurgery, along with remote sensing mechanisms to facilitate remote physical examinations. Effective use of these tools requires not only bandwidth and security, but also effective shared environments for communicating and working collaboratively with information about patients and resources. There is a strong overlap between this application need and crisis management, where the expertise and equipment for health care delivery may be damaged or remote from the crisis location.

NOTES

1. The Information Infrastructure Technology and Applications component of the federal High Performance Computing and Communications Initiative was formed in 1994 to promote research and development of technologies for a broadly accessible national information infrastructure. The Digital Libraries Initiative discussed in this chapter funds a range of projects related to information storage, discovery, integration, and retrieval.

2. The distinction between military and civilian crises does not necessarily extend to the mix of participants in a crisis response. For example, military personnel are frequently called upon to provide relief from natural disasters, and civilian relief organizations may be present in low-intensity military conflicts.

3. Sometimes mitigation is included by crisis managers as another stage of crisis management. Mitigation involves efforts to lessen the impact disasters have on people and property. Examples of mitigation include using zoning to keep homes away from floodplains, engineering bridges to withstand earthquakes, and enforcing effective building codes to protect property from hurricanes. Successful mitigation has the effect of reducing the impact of a crisis and perhaps keeping a situation from becoming a crisis. For a detailed case study, see FEMA (1993).

4. For further discussion of information technology costs, training needs, and usage patterns in civilian crisis management organizations, see Drabek (1991).

5. For detailed discussions of the importance of deployment and feedback from actual users in the design and development of information technologies, see Landauer (1995) and CSTB (1994a, pp. 181-184).

6. NCS is the primary agency responsible for communications functions in the Federal Response Plan for disasters. The study was conducted as part of a review of needs for a new service, the Emergency Response Link (ERLink), that the NCS is developing.

7. See also the NCS's GETS home page, http://164.117.147.223/~nc-pp/html/gets.htm.

8. Civilian relief agencies sometimes call upon U.S. military units to deploy similar capabilities.

9. Available from NI/USR home page, http://niusr.org/vision.html.

10. Whereas in a single organization it might be possible to dictate standards for interoperability, achieving agreement on standards is much more difficult when resources are owned and controlled by different organizations. This circumstance is increasingly common in many national-scale applications.

11. An interesting note on the impact of the regulatory policy environment on scientific experimentation is illustrated by the fact, reported by Egill Hauksson at Workshop II, that the California Institute of Technology (Caltech) was unable to deploy an experimental earthquake network for all of California, rather than just Southern California, because the network service donor, Pacific Bell, was unable to carry communications between the two halves of the state on its own networks. It would have to hand off the communications to a long-distance carrier, which as Hauksson noted, could have less direct incentive to support a public need in California than would a local firm such as Pacific Bell.

12. The Consequences Assessment Tool uses a model to predict damage from high winds that is adapted from a nuclear blast effects model developed by the Defense Nuclear Agency. The assessment tool is described in detail in Linz and Bryant (1994).

13. For additional details, see NOAA HPCC home page, http://hpcc1.hpcc.noaa.gov/hpcc.

14. Workshop participants observed that good judgments require not only access to information, but also a good general education on the part of judgment makers.

15. See Drabek (1991) for results of a detailed investigation of the relationship between training and information technology use in crisis management organizations.

16. Workshop series participant Clifford Lynch, Office of the President, University of California, made valuable contributions to this section. For a discussion of these research issues in greater depth and breadth, see Lynch and Garcia-Molina (1995).

17. The unpredictable timing of such demands highlights the potential benefit of continuous update of information in both GIS and digital libraries, or at least the incorporation of associated information (meta-data) about the currency and expected reliability of information.

18. Ordering and distribution of information-based (intangible) products can be nearly simultaneous, but the supporting accounting and inventory information, payment, and actual funds transfer may lag. The resulting decoupling of the accounting and payment information from the ordering and delivery of goods and services increases the credit risks associated with a transaction.

19. Each payment mechanism tends to work in a manner analogous to a physical mechanism such as credit cards, checks, or cash. Developing and deploying interoperable, seamless support for multiple payment mechanisms at an economically feasible cost is a challenge with both institutional aspects (e.g., negotiating contractual frameworks) and requirements for research.

20. Incorporation of video and sound into Web pages increases the richness of the content provided, but also increases the bandwidth required for access.

21. Networks among ATMs involve links with known and stable locations and relatively predictable load patterns (unlike the networks needed for crisis management).

22. For a more complete overview, see CSTB (1995b).

23. This illustrates what might be called "Amdahl's law for practical HPCC." For a classic discussion of key principles, see Amdahl (1967).

24. For a detailed description, see Syracuse University and Multidisciplinary Analysis and Design Industrial Consortium Team 2 (1995).

25. Workshop series participant Joel Saltz, of the University of Maryland, made valuable contributions to this section. For a discussion of these research issues in greater depth and breadth, see Davis et al. (1995).

26. For a discussion of medical record privacy issues in a networked environment, see IOM (1994).

27. Robots may find application in other elements of health care, such as handling and inspection of clinical or research specimens.

28. The current research frontier is petabyte-sized databases. An estimate from the NSF Workshop on High Performance Computing and Communications and Health Care (Davis et al., 1995) postulated that nationwide adoption of computerized patient records over the next decade will yield a full database size of 10 terabytes, which is well beyond current database management capabilities. This corresponds to the equivalent of 100 text pages for each of 100 million patients.

2

Technology: Research Problems Motivated by Application Needs

INTRODUCTION

Chapter 1 identifies opportunities to meet significant needs of crisis management and other national-scale application areas through advances in computing and communications technology. This chapter examines the fundamental research and development challenges those opportunities imply. Few of these challenges are entirely new; researchers and technologists have been working for years to advance computing and communications theory and technology, investigating problems ranging from maximizing the power of computation and communications capabilities to designing information applications that use those capabilities. What this discussion offers is a contemporary calibration, with implications for possible focusing of ongoing or future efforts, based on the inputs of technologists at the three workshops as well as a diverse sampling of other resources.

This chapter surveys the range of research directions motivated by opportunities for more effective use of technology in crisis management and other domains, following the same framework of technology areas—networking, computation, information management, and user-centered systems—developed in Chapter 1. Some of the directions address relatively targeted approaches toward making immediate progress in overcoming barriers to effective use of computing and communications, such as technologies to display information more naturally to people or to translate information more easily from one format to another. Others aim at gaining an understanding of coherent architectures and services that, when broadly deployed, could lead eventually to eliminating these barriers in a less ad hoc, more comprehensive fashion. Research on modeling the behavior of software systems composed from heterogeneous parts, for example, fits this category.

NETWORKING: THE NEED FOR ADAPTIVITY

Because of inherently unpredictable conditions, the communications support needed in a crisis must be adaptable; the steering committee characterizes the required capability as "adaptivity." Adaptivity involves making the best use of the available network capacity (including setting priorities for traffic according to needs and blocking out lower-priority traffic), as well as adding capacity by deploying and integrating new facilities. It also must support different kinds of services with fundamentally different technical demands, and to do so efficiently requires adaptivity. This section addresses specific areas for research in adaptive networks and describes the implications of a requirement for adaptivity; the importance of adaptivity at levels of information infrastructure above the network is discussed in other sections of this chapter.

Box 2.1 provides a sampling of networking research priorities discussed in the workshops. Although problems of networking that arise in national-scale applications are not entirely new, they require rethinking and redefinition because the boundaries of the problem domains are changing. Three issues that influence the scope of networking research problems are (1) scale, (2) interoperability, and (3) usability.

- *Scale.* High-performance networking is often thought of in terms of speed and bandwidth. Speed is limited, of course, by the speed of light in the transmission medium (copper, fiber, or air), and individual data bits cannot move over networks any faster. However, the overall speed of networks can be increased by raising the bandwidth (making the pipes wider and/or using more pipes in parallel) and reducing delays at bottlenecks in the network. High-speed networks (which include both high-bandwidth conduits or "pipes" and high-speed switching and routing) allow larger streams of data to traverse the network from point A to point B in a given amount of time. This makes possible the transmission of longer individual messages such as data files, wider signals (such as full-motion video), and greater numbers of messages (such as data integrated from large numbers of distributed sensors) over a given path at the same time. Research challenges related to the operation of high-speed networks include high-speed switching, buffering, error control, and similar needs; these were investigated with significant progress in the Defense Advanced Research Project Agency's (DARPA's) gigabit network testbeds.

    Speed and bandwidth are not the only performance challenges related to scale; national-scale applications must also scale in size. The number of information sources involved in applications may meet or even far exceed the size of the nation's or world's population. In theory, every information producer may be an information consumer and vice versa. Consequently, there is the need not only to reduce the amount of time needed for quantities of bits to be moved but, even at the limits of technology in increasing that speed, to transport more bits to more places. The set of people, workstations, databases, and computation platforms on networks is growing rapidly. Sensors are a potential source of even faster growth in the number of end points; as crisis management applications illustrate, networks may have to route bits to and from environmental sensors, seismometers, structural sensors on buildings and bridges, security cameras in stores and automated teller machines, and perhaps relief workers wearing cameras and other sensors on their clothes, rendering them what Vinton Cerf, of MCI Telecommunications Corporation, called "mobile multimodal sensor nets." Medical sensors distributed at people's homes, doctor's offices, crisis aid stations, and other locations may enable health care delivery in a new, more physically distributed fashion, but only if networks can manage the increased number of end points. In

---

BOX 2.1 SELECTED NETWORKING RESEARCH PRIORITIES SUGGESTED BY WORKSHOP PARTICIPANTS

- Daniel Duchamp, Columbia University:

  - Priority
  - High-bandwidth and/or frequent upstream communication
  - Bandwidth allocation that permits sudden, very large reallocations
  - Self-organizing routing structures
  - End point identification by attributes rather than just by name
  - Ease of use
  - Elimination of the concept of administrator

  Rajeev Jain, University of California, Los Angeles:

- Portable high-bandwidth radio modems that interface with portable computers and can be powered off the computer battery—these should be adaptable and interoperable with different frequency bands, channel conditions, and capacity requirements.
- Peer-to-peer distributed network protocols for setting up networks in the absence of wireline backbones.
- Bandwidth-efficient transmissions that allow increased capacity—for example, in many crises like the Northridge earthquake or Hurricane Andrew, even people in the same neighborhood were cut off due to the breakdown of telephone service. A portable bandwidth-efficient battery-operated peer-to-peer network technology would allow information systems to be set up to provide important support to communities in a crisis.

response, the communications infrastructure must be prepared to transport orders of magnitude more data and information and to handle orders of magnitude more separate addresses.

A particular case, such as a response to a single disaster, may not involve linking simultaneously to millions or billions of end points, but because the specific points that will be linked are not known in advance, the networking infrastructure must be able to accommodate the full number of names and addresses. The numbering plan of the public switched telecommunications network provides for this capability for point-to-point (voice circuit) calling under normal circumstances. In the broader context of all data, voice, and video communications, the Internet's distributed Domain Name Servers manage the numerical addresses that identify end points and names associated with those addresses. The explosive growth in Internet usage has motivated a change in the standard, Internet Protocol version 6, to accommodate more addresses.[1]

- *Interoperability*. The need for successfully communicating across boundaries in heterogeneous, long-lived, and evolving environments cannot be ignored. In crisis management, voice communications are necessary but not sufficient; response managers and field workers must be able to mobilize data inputs and more fully developed information (knowledge) from an enormous breadth of existing sources—some of them years old—in many forms. Telemedicine similarly requires a mix of communications modes, although not always over as unpredictable an infrastructure as crises present. Interoperation is more than merely passing waveforms and bits successfully; interoperation among the supporting services for communications, such as security and access priority, is highly complex when heterogeneous networks interconnect.

- *Usability*. The information and communications infrastructure is there to provide support to people, not just computers. In national-scale applications, nonexperts are increasingly important users of communications, making usability a crucial issue. What is needed are ways for people to use technology more effectively to communicate, not only with computers and other information sources and tools, but also with other people. Collaboration between people includes many modes of telecommunication: speech, video, passing data files to one another, sharing a consensus view of a document or a map. In crises, for example, the ability to manage the flow of communications among the people and machines involved is central to the enterprise and cannot be reserved solely to highly specialized technicians. Users of networks must be able to configure their communications to fit their organizational demands, not the reverse. This requirement implies far more than easy-to-use human-computer interfaces for network management software; the network itself must be able to adapt actively to its users and whatever information or other resources they need to draw upon.

For networks to be adaptive, they must be able to function during or recover quickly from unusual and challenging circumstances. The unpredictable damage and disruption caused by a crisis constitute challenging circumstances for which no specific preparations can be made. Unpredicted changes in a financial or medical network, such as movement of customers or a changing business alliance among insurers and hospitals that exchange clinical records, may also require adaptive response. Mobility—of users, devices, information, and other objects in a network—is a particular kind of challenge that is relevant not only to crisis response, but also to electronic commerce with portable devices, telemedicine, and wireless inventory systems in manufacturing, among others. Whenever the nodes, links, inputs, and outputs on a network move, that network must be able to adapt to change.

Randy Katz, of the University of California, Berkeley, has illustrated the demands for adaptivity of wireless (or, more generally, tetherless) networks for mobile computing in the face of highly diverse requirements with the example of a multimedia terminal for a firefighter (Katz, 1995). The device might be used in many ways: to access maps and plan routes to a fire; examine building blueprints for tactical planning; access databases locating local fire hydrants and nearby fire hazards such as chemical plants; communicate with and display the locations of other fire and rescue teams; and provide a location signal to a central headquarters so the firefighting team can be tracked for broader operational planning. All of the data cannot be stored on the device (especially because some data may have to be updated during the operation), so real-time access to centrally located data is necessary. The applications require different data rates and different trade-offs between low delay (latency) and freedom from transmission errors. Voice communications, for example, must be real time but can tolerate noisy signals; users can wait a few seconds to receive a map or blueprint, but errors may make it unusable. Some applications, such as voice conversation, require symmetrical bandwidth; others, such as data access and location signaling, are primarily one way (the former toward the mobile device, the latter away from it).

Research issues in network adaptivity fall into a number of categories, discussed in this section: self-organizing networks, network management, security, resource discovery, and virtual subnetworks. For networks to be adaptive, they must be easily reconfigurable either to meet different requirements from those for which they were originally deployed or to work around partial failures. In many cases of partial failures, self-configuring networks might discover, analyze, work around, and perhaps report failures, thereby achieving some degree of fault tolerance in the network. Over short periods, such as the hours after a disaster strikes, an adaptive network should restore services in a way that best utilizes the surviving infrastructure, enables additional resources to be integrated as they become available, and gives priority to the most pressing emergency needs. Daniel Duchamp, of Columbia University, observed, "Especially if the crisis is some form of disaster, there may be little or no infrastructure (e.g., electrical and telephone lines, cellular base stations) for two-way communication in the vicinity of an action site. That which exists may be overloaded. There are two approaches to such a problem: add capacity and/or shed load. Adding capacity is desirable but may be difficult; therefore, a mechanism for load shedding is desirable. Some notion of priority is typically a prerequisite for load shedding."

Networks can be adaptive not only to sharp discontinuities such as crises, but also to rapid, continuous evolution over a longer time scale, one appropriate to the pattern of growth of new services and industries in electronic commerce or digital libraries. The Internet's ability to adapt to and integrate new technologies, such as frame relay, asynchronous transfer mode (ATM), and new wireless data services, among many others, is one example.

Self-Organisation

Self-organizing networks facilitate adaptation when the physical configuration or the requirements for network resources have changed. Daniel Duchamp cast the problem in terms of an alternative to static operation:

> Most industry efforts are targeted to the commercial market and so are focused on providing a communications infrastructure whose underlying organization is static (e.g., certain sites are routers and certain sites are hosts, always). Statically organized systems ease the tasks of providing security and handling accounting/billing. Most communication systems are also pre-optimized to accommodate certain traffic patterns; the patterns are in large part predictable as a function of intra- and inter-business organization. It may be difficult or impossible to establish and maintain a static routing and/or connection establishment structure, because (1) hosts may move relative to each other, and (2) hosts, communication links, or the propagation environment may be inherently unstable. Therefore, a dynamically "self-organizing" routing and/or connection establishment structure is desirable.

Crisis management provides a compelling case for the need of networks to be self-organizing in order to create rapidly an infrastructure that supports communication and information sharing among workers and managers operating in the field. Police, fire, citizen's band, and amateur radio communications are commonly available in crises and could be used to set up a broadcast network, but they provide little support to manage peer-to-peer communications and make efficient use of the available spectrum. Portable, bandwidth-efficient peer-to-peer network technologies would allow information systems to be set up to support communications for relief workers. The issues of hardware development, peer-to-peer networking, and multimedia support are not limited to crisis management; they may be equally important to such fields as medicine and manufacturing (e.g., in networking of people, computers, and machine tools within a factory). Thus, research and development on self-organizing networks may be useful in the latter fields as well.

Rajeev Jain, of the University of California, Los Angeles, suggested two main deficiencies in terms of communications or networking technologies in a situation where relief officials arrive carrying laptop computers: (1) portable computing technology is not as well integrated with wireless communications technology as it should be, and (2) wireless communications systems still often rely on a wireline backbone for networking.[2] These factors imply that portable computers cannot currently be used to set up a peer-to-peer network if the backbone fails; radio modem technology has not yet advanced to a point where it can provide an alternative.[3] In mobile situations, people using portable computers need access to a wireline infrastructure to set up data links with another computer even if they are in close proximity. In addition, portable cellular phones cannot communicate with each other if the infrastructure breaks down. Jain concluded that both of these problems must be solved by developing technologies that better integrate portable computers with radio modems and allow peer-to-peer networks to be set up without wireline backbones, by using bandwidth-efficient transmission technologies.

Peer-to-peer networking techniques involve network configuration, multiple access protocols, and bandwidth management protocols. Better protocols need to be developed in conjunction with an understanding of the wireless communications technology so that bandwidth is utilized efficiently and the overhead of self-organization does not reduce the usable bandwidth drastically (the current situation in packet radio networks). Bandwidth is at a premium because of the large volume of information required in a crisis and because, although data and voice networks can be deployed using portable wireless technology, higher and/or more flexibly usable bandwidths are needed to support video communication. For example, images can convey vital information much more quickly than words, which can be important in crises or remote telemedicine. If paramedics need to communicate a diagnostic image of a patient (such as an electrocardiogram or x-ray) to a physician at a remote site and receive medical instructions, the amount of data that must be sent exceeds the capabilities of most wireless data communications technologies for portable computers. Technologies are now emerging that support data transmission rates in the tens of kilobits per second, which is sufficient for still pictures but not for full-motion video of more than minimal quality. A somewhat higher bandwidth capability could support a choice between moderate-quality full-motion video and high-quality images at a relatively low image or frame rate (resulting in jerky apparent motion). Another example relates to the usefulness of broadcasting certain kinds of data, such as full-motion video images of disaster conditions from a helicopter to workers in the field; traffic helicopters of local television stations often serve this function. However, if terrestrial broadcast capabilities are disabled, it could be valuable to use a deployable peer-to-peer network capability to disseminate such pictures to many recipients, potentially by using multicast technology.

The statement of James Beauchamp, of the U.S. Commander in Chief, Pacific Command, quoted in Chapter 1 underscored the low probability that all individuals or organizations involved in a crisis response will have interoperable radios (voice or data), especially in an international operation or one in which groups are brought together who have not trained or planned together before. Self-organizing networks that allowed smooth interoperation would be very useful in civilian and military crisis management and thus could have a high payoff for research. The lack of such technologies may be due partly to the absence of commercial applications requiring rapid configuration of wireless communications among many diverse technologies.

One purpose of the Department of Defense's (DOD's) Joint Warrior Interoperability Demonstrations (JWIDs; discussed in Chapter 1) is to test new technologies for bridging gaps in interoperability of communications equipment. The SpeakEasy technology developed at Rome Laboratory, for example, is scheduled to be tested in an operational exercise in the summer of 1996 during JWID '96.[4] SpeakEasy is an effort sponsored by DARPA and the National Security Agency to produce a radio that can emulate a multitude of existing commercial and military radios by implementing previously hardware-based waveform-generation technologies in software. Such a device should be able to act as if it were a high-frequency (HF) long-range radio, a very high frequency (VHF) air-to-ground radio, or a civilian police radio. Managing a peer-to-peer network of radios that use different protocols, some of which can emulate more than one protocol, is a complex problem for network research that could yield valuable results in the relatively near term.

Network Management

Network management helps deliver communications capacity to whoever may need it when it is needed. This may range from more effective sharing of network resources to priority overrides (blocking all other users) as needed. Network management schemes must support making decisions and setting priorities; it is possible that not all needs will be met if there simply are not enough resources, but allocations must be made on some basis of priority and need. Experimentation is necessary to understand better the architectural requirements with respect to such aspects as reliability, availability, security, throughput, connectivity, and configurability.

A network manager responding to a crisis must determine the state of the communications infrastructure. This means identifying what is working, what is not, and what is needed and can be provided, by taking into account characteristics of the network that can and should be maintained. For example, the existing infrastructure may provide some level of security. Then it must be determined whether it is both feasible and reasonable to continue to provide that level of security. Fault tolerance and priorities for activities are other characteristics of the network that must similarly be resolved.

In addition to network management tools to assess an existing situation, tools are needed to incorporate new requirements into the existing structure. For example, there may be great variability in the direction of data flow into and out of an area in which a crisis has occurred—for example, between command posts and field units. During some phases, remote units may be used for data collection to be transmitted to centralized or command facilities that in turn will need only lower communication bandwidth to the mobile units.

Adaptive network management can help increase the capability of the network elements, for example, by making the communications and computation able to run efficiently with respect to power consumption. Randy Katz has observed that wireless communication removes only one of the tethers on mobile computing; the other tether is electrical power (Katz, 1995). Advances in lightweight, long-lived battery technology and hardware technologies, such as low-power circuits, displays, and storage devices, would improve the performance of portable computers in a mobile setting. A possibility that is related directly to network management is the development of schemes that adapt to specific kinds of communications needs and incorporate broadcast and asymmetric communications to reduce the number and length of power-consuming transmissions by portable devices. For example, Katz observes that if a mobile device's request for a particular piece of information need not be satisfied immediately, the request can be transmitted at low power and low bandwidth. The response can be combined with those to other mobile devices, which are broadcast periodically to all of the units together at high power and bandwidth from the base stations. If a particular piece of information such as weather data is requested repeatedly by many users, it can be rebroadcast frequently to eliminate the need for remote units to transmit requests.

Priority policy is a critical issue in many applications; the need for rapid deployment and change in crisis management illustrates the issue especially clearly. Priority policy is the set of procedures and management principles implemented in a network to allocate resources (e.g., access to scarce communications bandwidth) according to the priority of various demands for those resources. Priority policy may be a function of the situation, the role of each participant, their locations, the content being transmitted, and many other factors. The dynamic nature of some crises may be reflected in the need for dynamic reassignment of such priorities. The problem is that one may have to change the determination of which applications (such as life-critical medical sensor data streams) or users (such as search and rescue workers) have priority in using the communications facilities. Borrowing resources in a crisis may require reconfiguring communications facilities designed for another use, such as local police radio. A collection of priority management issues must be addressed:

- Who has the authority to make a determination about priorities?
- How are priorities determined?
- How are priorities configured? Configuration needs to be secure, but also

user friendly, because the people performing it may not be network or communications experts.
- How are such priorities provided by the network and related resources?
- How will the network perform under the priority conditions assigned?

The last is a particularly difficult problem for network management. Michael Zyda, of the Naval Postgraduate School, identified predictive modeling of network latency as a difficult research challenge for distributed virtual environments, for which realistic simulation experiences set relatively strict limits on the latency that can be tolerated, implying a need for giving priority to those data streams.

One suggestion arising in the workshops was a priority server within a client-server architecture to centralize and manage evolving priorities. This approach might allow for the development of a multilevel availability policy analogous to a multilevel security policy. A dynamically configurable mechanism for allocating scarce bandwidth on a priority basis could enable creation of the "emergency lane" over the communications infrastructure that crisis managers at the workshops identified as a high-priority need. If such mechanisms were available they could be of great use in managing priority allocation in other domains such as medicine, manufacturing, and banking. In situations that are not crises, however, one might be able to plan ahead for changes in priority, and it is likely that network and communications expertise might be more readily available.

Victor Frost, of the University of Kansas, discussed the challenges of meeting diverse priority configuration within a network that integrates voice with other services:

> Some current networks use multilevel precedence (MLP) to ensure that important users have priority access to communications services. The general idea for MLP-like capabilities is that during normal operations the network satisfies the performance requirements of all users, but when the network is stressed, higher-priority users get preferential treatment. For voice networks, MLP decisions are straightforward: accept, deny, or cut off connections.
>
> However, as crisis management starts to use integrated services (i.e., voice, data, video, and multimedia), MLP decisions become more complex. For example, in today's systems an option is to drop low-precedence calls. In a multimedia network, not all calls are created equal. For example, dropping a low-precedence voice call would not necessarily allow for the connection of a high-precedence data call. MLP-like services should be available in future integrated networks. Open issues include initially allocating and then reallocating network resources in response to rapidly changing conditions in an MLP context. In addition, the infrastructure must be capable of transmitting MLP-like control information (signaling) that can be processed along with other network signaling messages. There is a need to develop MLP-like services that match the characteristics of integrated networks.

An ability to configure priorities, however, will require a much better understanding of what users actually need. Victor Frost also observed,

> Unfortunately, defining application-level performance objectives may be elusive. For example, users would always want to download a map or image instantaneously, but would they accept a [slower] response? A 10-minute response time would clearly be unacceptable for users directly connected to a high-speed network; but is this still true for users connected via performance-disadvantaged wireless links? . . . Performance-related deficiencies of currently available computing and communications capabilities are difficult to define without user-level performance specifications.

Security

Security is essential to national-scale applications such as health care, manufacturing, and electronic commerce. It also is important to crisis management, particularly in situations where an active adversary is involved or sensitive information must be communicated. Many traditional ideas of network security must be reconsidered for these applications in light of the greater scale and diversity of the infrastructure and the increased role of nonexperts.

To begin with, the nature of security policies may evolve. Longer-term research on new models of composability of policies will be needed as people begin to communicate more frequently with other people whom they do not know and may not fully trust. On a more short-term basis, new security models are needed to handle the new degree of mobility of users and possibly organizations. The usability or user acceptability of security mechanisms will assume new importance, especially those that inconvenience legitimate use too severely. New perspectives may be required on setting the boundaries of security policies not based on physical location.

Composability of Security Policies

As organizations and individuals form and re-form themselves into new and different groupings, their security policies must also be adapted to the changes. Three reorganization models—partitioning, subsumption, and federation—may be used, and each may engender changes in security policies. The following are simplistic descriptions, but they capture the general nature of changes that may occur. Partitioning involves a divergence of activity where unanimity or cooperation previously existed. In terms of security, partitioning does not appear to introduce a new paradigm or new problems. In contrast, subsumption and federation both involve some form of merging or aligning of activities and policies. Subsumption implies that one entity plays a primary role, while at least one other assumes a secondary role. Federation, on the other hand, implies an equal partnering or relationship. Both subsumption and federation may require that security policies be realigned, while perhaps seeking ways to continue to support previous policies and mechanisms. Both models of joining may be found in crisis management, as local emergency services agencies provide radio networks that other organizations brought in from outside must interact with and/or assume control over.

If policies and mechanisms are to be subsumed, the problems for security become significantly more difficult to address than in the past. In this case, if a unified top-level policy is to be enforced that is a composite of several others, interfaces among them—or, more abstractly, definitions of the policies, abstraction, and modularity—will be necessary to allow for exchange in controlled and well-known ways. It is only through such formal definitions that the composition of such activities can be sufficiently trustable to allow for the provision of a top-level composite of security policies and mechanisms.

A perhaps even more difficult problem is peer-level interaction within a federated model, in which neither domain's security policy takes clear precedence over the other. Such interaction will become more common as alliances are formed among organizations and individuals who are widely distributed. As virtual networks are set up in conjunction with temporary relationships, there is a continued need for security during any coordinated activities within the affiliation. Thus, the security mechanisms required by each participant must collaborate in ways that do not impede the coordination of their activities. Since there is no domination model in this case, coordination and compromise may be necessary. Again, these problems will be helped by research that provides better modularity and abstraction in order to formalize the relationships and interactions.

Mobility of Access Rights

In many, perhaps all, of the national-scale applications, users can be expected to move from one security policy domain or sphere to another and have a need to continue to function (e.g., carrying a portable computer from the wireless network environment of one's employer into that of a customer, supplier, or competitor). In some cases, the mobile user's primary objective will be to interact with the new local environment; in others, it will be to continue activities within the original or home domain. Most likely, the activities will involve some of both. In the first case, the user can be given a completely new identity with accruing security privileges in the new environment; alternatively, an agreement can be reached between the two domains, such that the new one trusts the old one to some degree, using that as the basis for any policy constraints on the user. This requires reciprocal agreements of trust between any relevant security domains. It is even possible to envisage cascading such trust, in either a hierarchical trust model or something less structured in which a mesh of trust develops with time, supporting transitive trust among domains. There is significant work to be done in such an area.

Mobile users who want to connect back to their home domain from a foreign one also have several alternatives. It is likely that the local domain will require some form of authentication and authorization of users. The remote domain might either accept that authentication, based on some form of mutual trust between the domains, or require separate, direct authentication and authorization from the user. In addition, such remote access may raise problems of exposure of activities, such as lack of privacy, greater potential for masquerading and spoofing, or denial of service, because all communication must now be transported through environments that may not be trusted.

If the user is trying to merge activities in the two environments, it is likely that a merged authentication and authorization policy will be the only rational solution. It is certainly imaginable that such a merged or federated policy might still be implemented using different security mechanisms in each domain, as long as the interfaces to the domains are explicit so that a composite can be created.

Usability of Security Mechanisms

Usability in a security context means not only that both system and network security must be easy for the end users (such as rescue workers or bank customers and officers) to use, but also that the exercise of translation from policy into configuration must be achievable by people in the field who are defining the policies and who may not be security experts. If security systems cannot be used and configured easily by people whose main objectives are completing other tasks, the mechanisms will be subverted. According to Daniel Duchamp, "Two obvious points . . . need considerable work. First, for disasters especially, technology should intrude as little as possible on the consciousness of field workers. Second, all goals should be achieved without the need for system administrators." Users often do not place a high priority on the security of the resources they are using, because the threats do not weigh heavily against the objective of achieving some other goal. Thus, the cost (including inconvenience) to these users must be commensurate with the perceived level of utility. As Richard Entlich, of the Institute for Defense Analyses, observed, "Creating a realistic way of providing security at each node involves not only technical issues, but a change in operational procedures and user attitudes." Ideally, technological designs and approaches should reinforce those needed changes on the part of users.

Unfortunately, the problems of formulating security policy are even more difficult to address with computational and communications facilities. Policy formation, especially when it involves merging several different security domains, is extremely complex. It must be based on the tasks to be achieved, the probability of subversion if security policy constraints are too obstructive, and the capabilities of the mechanisms available, especially when merging of separate resources is necessary.

Discovery of Resources

Crisis management highlights the need for rapid resource discovery. Resources may be electronic, such as information or services, or they may be more tangible, such as computers, printers, and wires used in networks. First, one must determine what resources are needed. Then, perhaps with help from information networks, one might be able to discover which resources are local and, if those are inadequate, whether some remote resources may be able to address an otherwise insoluble problem. An example of this latter situation would be finding an expert on an unusual bacterial infection that appears to have broken out in a given location.

In crises, some of the tools mentioned above for network management and reorganization in the face of partial failures may also help to identify which local computing, communications, and networking resources are functional. If high-performance computing is necessary for a given task, such as additional or more detailed weather forecasting or geological (earthquake) modeling, discovering computing and network facilities that are remote and accessible via adequately capable network connections might be invaluable.

Virtual Subnetworks

Another architectural requirement common to several of the application areas is the ability to create virtual subnetworks. The virtual "subnet" feature allows communities to be created for special purposes. For example, in manufacturing, the creation of a virtual subnet for a company and its subcontractors might simplify the building of applications by providing a shared engineering design tool. It would allow a global or national corporation to operate as though it had a private subnet. It might provide similar features for any community, such as a network of hospitals that has a need to exchange patient records.

A virtual subnet will appear to applications and supporting software as if communications are happening on a separate network that actually is configured within a larger one. In essence, the virtual subnet capability allows a policy or activity boundary concept to be made evident in the network model as a subnet. At present, virtual subnets are generally used to reflect administrative domains in which a single consistent set of usage and access policies is enforced.

The possibility of defining a subnet for crisis management in terms of security and priority access has already been suggested. Another potentially useful way to define a boundary around a subnet would be to control the flow of information passing into that subnet by using priority-based filtering mechanisms. This would be done to reserve scarce bandwidth and storage within the subnet for only the most valuable information.

In order to make virtual subnets useful, there must be automated ways of creating them within the Internet or the broader national or global information infrastructure. This implies understanding the policies to be enforced on such a subnet with respect to, for example, usage and security, and being able to both recognize and requisition resources to create and manage subnets. It may mean provision of various services within the network in such a way that those services can be provided effectively to subnets. Examples of these might be trusted encryption services, firewalls, protocol conversion gateways, and others. A virtual subnet must have all the characteristics of a physical subnet, while allowing its members to be widely distributed physically.[5]

By providing application- or user-level community boundary models down into the network, one might create a more robust, survivable environment in which to build applications. Both advances in technology development and more fundamental research on architectural models for subnets are needed to automate support for creating such subnets in real time and on a significantly larger scale than is currently supported.

COMPUTATION: DISTRIBUTED COMPUTING

The networked computational and mass storage resources needed for national-scale application areas are necessarily heterogeneous and geographically distributed. A geographically remote, accessible metacomputing resource, as envisioned in the Crisis 2005 scenario in Chapter 1, implies network-based adaptive links among available people (using portable computers and communications, such as personal digital assistants) to large-scale computation on high-performance computing platforms. The network connecting these computing and storage resources is the enabling technology for what might be termed a network-intensive style of computation. Allen Sears, of DARPA, summarized this idea as "the network is the computer"; that is, computation to address a user's problem may routinely take place out on a network, somewhere other than the user's location.

Crisis management is a good example of a network-intensive application. People responding to crises could benefit from larger-scale mass storage and higher computation rates than are typically available in the field, for example, to gain the benefits of high-performance simulation performed away from the crisis location.[6] The technical implication of network-intensive computing for crisis management is not merely a massive computational capability, but rather an appropriately balanced computing and communications hierarchy. This would integrate computing, storage, and data communications across a scale from lightweight portable computers in the field to remote, geographically distributed high-performance computation and mass storage systems for database and simulation support. Research in many areas, such as mobility and coordination of resources and management of distributed computing, is needed to achieve this balanced hierarchy.

Modeling and Simulation

High-performance computation may be used to simulate complex systems, both natural and man-made, for many applications. Networks can make high-performance computation resources remotely accessible, enabling sharing of expensive resources among users throughout the nation. Applications of modeling and simulation to crisis management include the prediction of severe storms, flooding, wildfire evolution, toxic liquid and gas dispersion, structural damage, and other phenomena. As discussed in Chapter 1, higher-quality predictions than are available today could save lives and reduce the cost of response significantly.

Grand Challenge activities under the High Performance Computing and Communications Initiative (HPCCI) have been a factor in advancing the state of the art of modeling and simulation (CSTB, 1995a; OSTP, 1993, 1994a; NSTC, 1995). The speed of current high-performance simulation for many different applications, however, continues to need improvement. Lee Holcomb, of the National Aeronautics and Space Administration (NASA), observed, for example, that it is currently infeasible for long-term climate change models to involve the coupling of ocean and atmospheric effects, because of inadequate speed of the models for simulating atmospheric effects (which change much more rapidly than ocean effects and therefore must be modeled accordingly). In addition, whereas fluid dynamics models are able to produce very nice pictures of airflow around aircraft wings and to calculate lift, they are not able to model drag accurately, which is the other basic flight characteristic required in aircraft design. Holcomb summarized, "We have requirements that go well beyond the current goals of the High Performance Computing Program."

The urgency of crises imposes a requirement that may pertain more strictly in crisis management than in other applications such as computational science: the ability to run simulations at varying scales of resolution is crucial to being able to make appropriate trade-offs between the accuracy of the prediction and the affordability and speed of the response. Kelvin Droegemeier, of the University of Oklahoma, described work on severe thunderstorm modeling at the university's Center for the Analysis and Prediction of Storms (CAPS), including field trials in 1995 that demonstrated the ability to generate and deliver high-performance modeling results within a time frame useful to crisis managers. For areas within 30 km of a Doppler radar station, microscale predictions have been made at a 1-km scale and can predict rapidly developing events, such as microbursts, heavy rain, hail, and electrical buildup, on 10- to 30-minute time scales. At scales of 1 to more than 10 km, the emergence and intensity of new thunderstorms, cloud ceiling, and visibility have been predicted up to two hours in advance, and the evolution (e.g., movement, change in intensity) of existing storms has been forecast three to six hours in advance. Rescaling the model thus allows greater detail to be generated where it is most needed, in response to demands from the field.[7]

As Droegemeier noted, time is critical for results to be of operational value:

> These forecasts are only good for about six hours. This means you have to collect the observational data, primarily from Doppler radars; retrieve from these data various quantities that cannot be observed directly; generate an initial state for the model; run the model; generate the forecast products; and make forecast decisions in a time frame of 30 to 60 minutes because otherwise, you have eaten up a good portion of your forecast period. It is a very timely problem that absolutely requires high-performance computing and communications. If you can't predict the weather significantly faster than it evolves, then the prediction is obviously useless.

When high performance is required, adding complexity at various scales of prediction may not be worth the cost in time or computer resource usage. For example, the CAPS storm model could predict not only the presence of hail, but the average size of the hailstones; however, the cost is probably beyond what one would be willing to pay computationally to have that detail in real time. Because the model's performance scales with added computing capacity, more detailed predictions can in principle be made if enough computational resources can be coordinated to perform them.[8]

Crisis managers also require a sense of the reliability of data they work with-the "error bars" around simulation results. To achieve this, an ensemble of simulations may be run using slightly different initial conditions. Ensemble simulation is especially important for chaotic phenomena, where points of great divergence from similar input conditions may not be readily apparent. Ensemble simulation is ideally suited for running in parallel, because the processes are essentially identical and do not communicate with or influence each other. The difficult problem is identifying how to alter the initial conditions. As Droegemeier noted, Monte Carlo simulation optimizes these variations to give the best results, but depends on a knowledge of the natural variability of the modeled phenomena that is not always available (e.g., in the case of severe thunderstorm phenomena at the particular scales CAPS is modeling). The infrequency of large crises makes it difficult to gain this understanding of natural variability in some cases. More broadly, it impedes verifying models of extraordinary events. As Robert Kehlet, of the Defense Nuclear Agency, said, "We are in the awkward position of not wanting to have to deal with a disaster, but needing a disaster to be able to verify and validate our models."

Besides resources to perform the computations, remote modeling and simulation also implies the need for adequate network capability to transport input data to the model and distribute results to the scene. Input data collection requirements may be most demanding if large amounts of real-time sensor data are involved (see the section "Sensors and Data Collection" below). Sensors will ideally send compressed digitized data in packets that are compatible with existing high-speed networks. However, the observation by Egill Hauksson, of the California Institute of Technology, that high-speed network costs remain too high for nonexperimental applications suggests that additional network research and deployment could be necessary to make this a practical reality for crisis management.

Don Eddington, of the Naval Research and Development Center, outlined a model, tested in the JWID exercises, for performing and/or integrating the results of simulations at "anchor desks." Anchor desks, located away from the front line of crisis, could be staffed with people expert at running and interpreting simulations, who could disseminate results to the field when conditions warrant (e.g., a major change in the situation is detected). This model reduces the amount of network traffic below that required by full-time connection from the field to the remote high-performance computing platform. Distributing results can be done by simply distributing a map or picture of the simulation result.

However, if information is to be integrated with other data available to workers at the scene, or if complex three-dimensional visualizations of the results are called for, a picture or map may not suffice and a complete data file must be sent. (Needs for information integration and display are discussed in the next two sections.) This implies higher-bandwidth connections and greater display capabilities on the front line user's platform. Ultimately, finding the optimal balance of resources for various kinds of crises will require experimentation in training exercises and actual deployments. It should also be influenced by social science research on how crisis managers actually use information provided to them.

Mobility of Computation and Data

Efficiency and performance typically demand that a computation be carried out near its input and output data. Although the traditional solution is to move the data to the computation, sometimes the computation requires so much data so quickly that it is better to move the computation to the data. Since the appropriate software may not already reside on the target system, an executable or interpretable program may have to be transmitted across the network and executed remotely. This extends the meaning of the term relocatable beyond the ability of programmers to port code easily from one platform to another to the ability of code to operate in a truly platform-independent manner in response to urgent demands.

In some circumstances, achieving high performance requires that the application software be optimized specifically for the machine on which it is to operate, which usually requires recompilation of the application. For this approach to have the desired effect, the compilation environment must be able to tailor the application to the specific target machine. This tailoring will not work unless the application is written in a machine-independent implementation language and it can be compiled on each target machine to achieve performance comparable to the best possible on that machine using the same algorithm.

This problem—compiler and language support for machine-independent programming—is one of the key challenges in high-performance computation. Although languages such as High Performance Fortran (HPF) and standard interfaces like the Message Passing Interface (MPI) are excellent first steps for parallel computing, the machine-independent programming problem remains an important subject of continuing research. Comments from Lee Holcomb indicate that although progress has been made, research on machine-independent programming remains crucial to high-performance computing in all areas, not just crisis management:

> I think [programming for high-performance computing] is getting better. I think many of the machines coming out today, as opposed to the ones that were produced, say, a year and a half to two years ago, provide a much better environment. But when you ask a lot of computational scientists, who have spent their whole life porting the current [code] over to one machine and then on to the next, when you give them the third machine to port it over to and have to retune it, they lose a lot of interest and enthusiasm.

An ability to relocate computation rapidly will require dynamic binding of code at run time to common software and system services (e.g., input-output, storage access). This implies a need for further development and standardization of those services (e.g., through common application programming interfaces; APIs) such that software can be written to take advantage of them.

However, software applications that were not originally written to be relocatable may require a wrapper to translate their interfaces for the remote system. In manufacturing applications, such wrappers are prewritten, which is often a costly, labor-intensive process. Research on generic methods enabling more rapid construction of wrappers for software applications—ultimately, producing them "on the fly," as might be required in a crisis—was identified by workshop participants as potentially valuable but currently quite challenging. Advances in wrapper generation for software applications would enable more reuse of software and would benefit many areas in addition to crisis management. However, such advances will require basic research leading to an ability to model, predict, and reason about software systems composed of heterogeneous parts that is far beyond current capabilities. These advances could be more generally relevant to many aspects of software systems, as discussed below in the section "Software System Development."

Storage Servers and Meta-Data

Crisis management applications employ databases of substantial size. For example, workshop participants estimated that a database of the relevant infrastructure (e.g., utilities, building plans) of Los Angeles requires about 2 terabytes. Not all of it must be handled by any one computer at one time; however, all of it may potentially have to be available through the response organization's distributed communications. In addition, a wide variety of data formats and representations occur and must be handled; this may always be the case because of the unpredictability of some needs for data in a crisis. Reformatting data rapidly through services such as those discussed in the section "Information Management" can be computationally intensive and require fast storage media.

Comprehensive provisions must also be made for storing not only data, but collateral information (meta-data) needed to interpret the data. Besides concerns appropriate to all distributed file systems (authentication, authorization, naming, and the like), these involve issues of data validity, quality, and timeliness, all of which are needed for reliable use of the data, and semantic self-description to support integration and interoperability.

To customize information handling for particular applications, storage server software should be able to interpret and respond to the meta-data. Workshop participants suggested that in crisis management, for example, a scheme could be developed to use meta-data to limit the use of scarce bandwidth and to minimize storage media access time while accommodating incoherence of data distributed throughout the response organization. To conserve bandwidth, a central database system located outside the immediate crisis area could maintain a copy of the information stored in each computer at the scene of the crisis. Instead of replicating whole databases across the network when new information alters, contradicts, or extends the information in either copy, a more limited communication could take place to restore coherence between copies or at least provide a more consistent depiction of the situation. A "smart" coherence protocol could relay only changes in the data, or perhaps an executable program to accomplish them. Relevant meta-data for making these determinations might include, for example, time of last update for each data point, so that new data can be identified, and an estimate of quality, to avoid replacing older but "good" data with newer "less good" data.

Besides resource conservation, a beneficial side effect of this coherence scheme would be the creation of a fairly accurate and up-to-date representation of the entire crisis situation, valuable for coordination and decision making. Modeling the coherence and flow of information into, within, and out of the crisis zone could be incorporated into a system that would continuously search for (and perhaps correct) anomalies and inconsistencies in the data. It could also support collaboration and coordination among the people working on a response operation by helping crisis managers know what information other participants have available to them.

Anomaly Detection and Inference of Missing Data

High-performance computing can be used for filling in missing data elements (through machine inference that they are part of a computer-recognizable pattern), information validation, and data fusion in many national-scale applications. For example, crisis data are often incomplete or simply contradictory. Simulation could be used to identify outlier data, flagging potential errors that should be verified. Higher computational performance is required to correct or reconstruct missing data from complex dynamic systems, interpolating information such as wind speeds and directions or floodwater levels through machine inference. Incorrect data—perhaps derived from faulty sensors, taken from out-of-date or incorrect databases, or deliberately introduced by an active adversary—could be detected and corrected by computers in situations where the complexity or volume of the data patterns would make it difficult for a human to notice the error. Ordinarily, the absence of key information requires users to make intuitive judgments; tools that help cope with gaps in information are one element of what workshop participants called "judgment support" (see the section "User-Centered Systems" below in this chapter).

The widespread presence of semantic meta-data could enhance data mining and inference for detecting errors in databases. Data mining in high-performance systems has been effective in other applications, for example, in finding anomalous credit card and medical claims; new applications such as clinical research are also anticipated (see Box 2.2). However, the nature of crises is such that data being examined for anomalies may be of an unanticipated nature and may not be fully understood. There is a challenge for research in identifying the right types of meta-data that could make data mining and inference over those unanticipated data possible.

Sensors and Data Collection

More widespread use of networked sensors could generate valuable inputs for crisis management, as well as remote health care and manufacturing process automation. The variety of potentially useful sensors is particularly broad in crisis management, including environmental monitors such as those deployed in the Oklahoma MesoNet or the NEXRAD (Next Generation Weather Radar) Doppler radar system; video cameras that have been installed to enhance security or monitor vehicle traffic; and structural sensors (as in "smart" buildings, bridges, and other structures networked with stress and strain sensors).

Some imagery, such as photographs of a building before it collapsed or satellite photographs showing the current extent of a wildfire, are potential input data for simulation. Timely access to and sharing of these data require high-performance communication, including network management, both to and from the crisis scene. Moreover, models could be designed to take real-time sensor inputs and modify their parameters accordingly to accomplish a more powerful capability to predict phenomena. As Donald Brown, of the University of Virginia, noted, the nonlinearity of many real-world phenomena poses challenges for modeling; learning how to incorporate these nonlinearities into models directly from sensors could improve the performance of models significantly.

BOX 2.2 CLINICAL RESEARCH APPLICATIONS OF DATA MINING

Historically, challenges posed by medical problems have motivated many advances in the fields of statistics and artificial intelligence. Traditionally, researchers in both fields have had to make do with relatively small medical datasets that typically consisted of no more than a few thousand patient records. This situation will change dramatically over the next decade, by which time we anticipate that most health care organizations will have adopted computerized patient record systems. A decade from now, we can expect that there will be some 100 million and eventually many more patient records with, for example, a full database size of 10 terabytes, corresponding to 100 text pages of information for each of 100 million patients. Functionalities needed in the use and analysis of distributed medical databases will include segmentation of medical data into typical models or templates (e.g., characterization of disease states) and comparison of individual patients with templates (to aid diagnosis and to establish canonical care maps). The need to explore these large datasets will drive research projects in statistics, optimization, and artificial intelligence. . . .

Care providers and managers will want to be able to rapidly analyze data extracted from large distributed and parallel databases that contain both text and image data. We anticipate that . . . significant performance issues . . . will arise because of the demand to interactively analyze large (multi-terabyte) datasets. Users will want to minimize waste of time and funds due to searches that reveal little or no relevant information in response to a query, or retrieval of irrelevant, incorrect or corrupted datasets.

SOURCE: Davis et al. (1995), as summarized at Workshop III by Joel Saltz, of the University of Maryland.

Sometimes a sensor designed for one purpose can be used opportunistically for another. For example, an addressable network of electric utility power usage monitors could be used to determine which buildings still have power after an earthquake, and which of those buildings with power are likely to have occupants. A similar approach could be taken using the resources of a residential network service provider. Workshop participants suggested that security cameras also provide opportunities for unusual use; with ingenuity it may be possible to estimate the amplitude and frequency of an earth tremor or the rate at which rain falls by processing video images. Given the high cost of dedicated sensor networks and the infrequency of crises, technology to better exploit existing sensors opportunistically could facilitate their use.

People carrying sensors might be another effective mode of sensor network deployment. Robert Kehlet noted that field workers could wear digital cameras on their helmets; personal geographic position monitors could be used to correlate the video data with position on a map. Physical condition monitors on workers in dangerous situations could hasten response if someone is injured.

Research is needed to optimize architectures for processing real-time information from large, highly scalable numbers of inputs.[9] The problem is likely amenable to parallel processing, as demonstrated on a smaller scale in research described by Jon Webb, of Carnegie Mellon University, on machine vision synthesized from large numbers of relatively inexpensive cameras. A highly decentralized architecture, perhaps using processors built into the sensors themselves (sometimes characterized as "intelligence within the network"), might be a highly effective way to conserve bandwidth and processing; sensors could detect from their neighbors whether a significant change in overall state is occurring and could communicate that fact to a central location, otherwise remaining silent. There could be value in research and development toward a network designed such that, in response to bandwidth or storage constraints in the network, discrete groups of sensors perform some data fusion before passing their data forward; an adaptive architecture could permit this feature to adjust to changing constraints and priorities.

Distributed Resource Management

Network-intensive computing places unusual stress on conventional computer system management and operation practice. Describing the general research challenge, Randy Katz said,

> We tend to forget about the fact that [the information infrastructure] won't be just servers and clients, information servers or data servers. There are going to be compute-servers or specialized equipment out there that can do certain functions for us. It will be interesting to understand what it takes to build applications that can discover that such special high-performance engines that exist out there can split off a piece of themselves, execute on it, and recombine when the computation is done.

Because significant remote computing and storage resources may be necessary, standardized services for resource allocation and usage accounting are important. Other important issues are enforcing the proper use of network resources, determining the scale and quality of service available, and establishing priorities among the users and uses. Mechanisms are needed to address these issues automatically and dynamically. Operating system resource management is weak in this area because it treats tasks more or less identically. For example, many current network-aware batch systems are configured and administered manually and support no rational network-wide basis for cost determination.

Dennis Gannon, of Indiana University, suggested the value of continued development of network resource management tools as follows: "High-performance computing . . . should be part of the fabric of the tools we use. It should be possible for a desktop applications at one site to invoke the resources of a supercomputer or a specialized computing instrument based on the requirements of the problem. A network resource request broker should provide cost-effective solutions based on the capabilities of compute servers." He pointed to the Information Wide-Area Year (I-WAY) experimental network as a useful early demonstration of such capabilities.[10]

Software System Development

To the extent that it improves capabilities for integrating software components as they relocate and interact throughout networks, research enabling a network-intensive style of computing may be helpful in addressing a long-standing, fundamental problem for many application areas, that of large software system development. Speaking about electronic commerce systems, Daniel Schutzer, of Citibank, said succinctly, "The programming bottleneck is still there." DARPA's Duane Adams described the problem as follows:

> Many of our application programs [at DARPA] are developing complex, software-intensive systems. For example, we are developing control systems for unmanned aerial vehicles (UAVs) that can fly an airplane for 24 or 36 hours at ranges of 3,000 miles from home; we are developing simulation-based design systems to aid in the design of a new generation of ships; and we are developing complex command and control systems. These projects are using very few of the advanced information technologies that are being developed elsewhere in [D]ARPA—new languages, software development methodologies and tools, reusable components. So we still face many of the same problems that we have had for years.
>
> This raises some interesting technology problems. Are we working on the right set of problems, and are we making progress? How do we take this technology and actually insert it into projects that are building real systems? I think one of the biggest challenges we face is building complex systems. We have talked about some of the problems. One of them is clearly a scaling problem . . . scaling to the number of processors in some of the massively parallel systems [and] . . . scaling software so you can build very large systems and incrementally build them, evolve them over time.

Software reuse through integration of existing components with new ones is necessary to avoid the cost of reproducing functionality for new applications from scratch. Building large systems often needs to be done rapidly, and because most large systems have a long, evolutionary lifetime, they must be designed to change. However, these are not easy challenges. Distributed object libraries such as those facilitated by the Common Object Request Broker Architecture (CORBA; discussed in the next section, "Information Management") may be useful, but more developed frameworks and infrastructure are needed to make them fully usable in the building of applications by large distributed teams of people. Basic tools to support scalable reuse, to catalogue and locate them, and to manage versioning are still primitive.

It is clear that getting even currently available system-building technologies and methods into actual use in the software development enterprise is a major challenge. Changing the work practices of organizations takes time; however, there may be ways in which collaboration technology can make it easier to incorporate the available techniques into work practices more smoothly. A collaboration environment that allows software development teams to manage the complex interactions among their activities could reap benefits across the spectrum of applications. Dennis Gannon identified the need to design a "problem-solving environment" technology that provides an infrastructure of tools to allow a distributed set of experts and users to build, for example, large and complex computer applications. Participants in Workshop I developed a subjective report card rating the current state of the art in computing environments as follows:

- Application construction (mixed expression, visual programming, groupware, portable and reusable parts—including how to finance them) D

- Execution control (management of scheduling and resources, data, performance) D

- Performance and data visualization B

- Debugging C+

- Testing C

- Application management (applications, databases, versioning) C

- Rapid prototyping (e.g., to evaluate look and feel) C−

In the absence of a deeper understanding of large, distributed software systems, however, new tools are not likely to improve the situation. Decades of experience with software engineering indicate that the problems are difficult—they are not solvable purely by putting larger teams of engineers to work or by making new tools and techniques available (CSTB, 1992, pp. 103-107; CSTB, 1989). Barbara Liskov, of the Massachusetts Institute of Technology, cited the need for a good model of distributed computation on which to develop systems and reason about their characteristics—a software infrastructure, not just a programming language or a collection of tools, that would support a way of thinking about programs, how they communicate, and their underlying memory model (see Box 2.3). A consistent software infrastructure model of computation could form the basis not only for building systems using that model but for reasoning about their correctness and performance as they are being built. It would be extremely useful for system developers to be able to predict the performance, fault tolerance, or other specified features of a system composed from parts whose properties are known.

BOX 2.3 CHALLENGES OF PROGRAMMING

At Workshop III, Barbara Liskov, of the Massachusetts Institute of Technology, observed:

"People have to write programs that run on these [large-scale, distributed] systems. Applications need to be distributed, and they have got to work, and they must do their job with the right kind of performance. . . . These applications are difficult to build. One of the things I was struck by in the conversations today was the very ad hoc way that people were thinking of building systems. It was just a bunch of stuff that you connect together—this component meshes with that component. You know, we can't build systems that way. And the truth is we hardly know how to build systems that worked on the old kind of distributed network. . . .

"We have a real software problem. If I want to build an application where I can reason about its correctness and its performance under a number of adverse conditions, what I need is a good model of computation on which to base that system, so that I have some basis for thinking about what it is doing. I think what we need is a software infrastructure, and I don't mean by this a programming language and I also don't mean some bag of tools that some manufacturers make available. I mean some way of thinking about what programs are, what their components are, where these components live, how they communicate, what kind of access they have to shared memory, what kind of model of memory it is, whether there is a uniform model, whether it is a model where different pieces of the memory have different fault tolerance characteristics, what is the fault tolerance model of the system as a whole, what kinds of atomicity guarantees are provided, and so on. We don't have anything approaching this kind of model for people to build their applications on today."

This problem of composability of software components is very difficult and requires fundamental research. Increased understanding, however, could support a valuable increase in the ability to build systems driven by application needs. Dennis Gannon said, "We should be able to have software protocols that would allow us to request a computing capability based on the problem specification, not based on machine architectures." This will be especially crucial as the stability of discrete machine architectures becomes less fixed with network-centered computing. For example, Vinton Cerf observed that in network-intensive computing, the buses of the traditional computer architecture are replaced in some respects with network links of a reliability that is unpredictable and often less than perfect. There must also be a way of representing the cost, reliability, and bandwidth trade-offs of various network links in a way that software can understand and act upon, so they can be optimized according to the needs of the problem at hand. These fundamental issues of computation represent a difficult but potentially very valuable avenue for investigation.

INFORMATION MANAGEMENT: FINDING AND INTEGRATING RESOURCES

In the past decade, there have been important transitions in information management technologies used in large organizations. This is usually characterized as a shift from centralized to more distributed resources, but perhaps a more accurate characterization is that it is a better balancing between centralized and distributed control of information production, location, and access. Technologies such as client-server architectures and distributed on-line transaction processing systems have enabled this more effective balancing. It is an ongoing activity at all levels of organization structure, from central databases to individual and group-specific resources.

This situation, difficult as it is within a single organization, becomes much more complex with the scale up to national, multiorganizational applications. This section considers the information management challenges posed by national-scale applications, with particular emphasis on crisis management. It examines several important issues and trends in information management and suggests additional challenges.

Information management involves a broad range of resources with different purposes, such as traditional databases (typically relational), digital libraries, multimedia databases (sometimes used in video servers), object request brokers (such as those in CORBA), wide-area file systems (such as the Network File System and Andrew File System), corporate information webs based on groupware and/or the World Wide Web, and others. Besides relational tables, conventional types of information objects can include multimedia objects (images, video, hypermedia), structured documents (possibly incorporating network-mobile, executable software components, or "applets"), geographical coordinate systems, and application- or task-specific data types. It is useful to classify these information management resources into four organizational categories: (1) central institutional resources, (2) individual desktop resources, (3) group resources, and (4) ubiquitous resources such as the communications network and e-mail service.

Central resources include institutional databases, digital libraries, and other centrally managed information stores. These typically have regular schemas; extensive support for concurrency and robust access; and supporting policy frameworks to maintain (or at least monitor) quality, consistency, security, completeness, and other attributes. Data models for institutional resources are evolving in several ways (such as the evolution from relational to object-relational databases), but these models are meant to support large-scale and uniform data management applications.

Individual resources consist of ad hoc structures. These resources may be in a process of evolving into more regular structures of broader value to an organization (a process often called upscaling). Alternatively, they may be individual resources that differentiate and provide a competitive edge to the individual and so are unlikely to be shared.

Group resources can include scaled-down and specialized institutional resources as well as ad hoc shared resources. This suggests a continuum from ad hoc ephemeral individual resources through group resources to robust managed institutional resources. Examples of group resources are engineering design repositories, software libraries, and partially formulated logistics plans.

The final class of resources, which may be called ubiquitous resources, consists of shared communications and information services on a communications network, including services such as electronic mail, newsgroups, and the World Wide Web. These services exist uniformly throughout an organization and, unlike the other classes of resources, generally do not reflect organizational hierarchy.

This classification of resources provides a useful framework for examining broad trends in information management and considering, particularly, the special problems associated with national-scale applications, such as the following:

1. *Information integration.* In many of these applications, information must be integrated with other information in diverse formats. This may include integration of diverse access control regimes to enable appropriate sharing of information while simultaneously maintaining confidentiality and integrity. It can also include integration of institutional, group, and personal information. Related to the integration problem is the issue of information location—how can information be indexed and searched to support national-scale applications?
2. *Meta-data and types.* Shared objects in very large-scale applications can have a rich variety of types, and these types can be very complex. An example of a family of complex types is the diversity of representations and formats for image information. How can objects be shared and used when their types are evolving, perhaps not at the same pace as the applications software that uses them? Also, there is an evolving view of information objects as aggregations of information, computation, and structure. How will this new view affect information management more broadly? Related to this is the more general issue of meta-data: descriptive information about data, including context (origin, ownership, etc.) as well as syntactic and semantic information. Meta-data approaches are needed that support modeling of quality and other attributes through an

integration process. This could include integration of information that may appear to be inconsistent due to quality problems.
3 . *Production and value.* A final information product can be derived through a series of steps involving multiple information producers and organizations. This involves addressing the development of models for the kinds of steps that add value to a product beyond the information integration problem mentioned above.
4 . *Distribution and relocation.* The linking of information resources at all levels into national-scale applications places great stress on a variety of distributed computing issues such as robustness and survivability, name management, and flexible networking. In addition, there is the issue of adaptivity—the interplay of network capability and applications behavior.

Before examining these four issues in greater detail, it is useful to point out some general trends in information management that are part of the evolution already under way to national-scale applications.

First, the ongoing shift over the past decade from central mainframe resources to more distributed client-server configurations is giving way to a steady migration of both resources and control over resources within organizations. This suggests that the main challenge is to better enable this shift as an ongoing process, rather than as a one-time effort. This steady flux is sustained by the emergence of ad hoc groups that establish and manage their own resources (which must later be integrated with others), by a continual change and improvement in information management technologies, and by structural change within organizations. A military joint task force and a civilian crisis action team are examples of ad hoc groups that both establish their own resources and rely on a broad range of institutional resources. In other words, we are just beginning to explore the interplay among institutional information resources, individual ad hoc information resources, and communications and information services such as electronic mail and the World Wide Web.

Second, the complexity and quantity of information, the range and diversity of sources, and the range of types and structures for information are all increasing rapidly, as is the need to assimilate and exploit information rapidly. The problem is not an overload of information, but rather a greater challenge to manage it effectively. Also, as noted above, the nature of the information items is changing: they have more explicit structure, more information about their type, more semantic information, and more computational content. There are also increasingly stringent requirements to manage intellectual property protection and support commerce in information items.

Finally, there is greater interconnectivity and heterogeneity both within and among organizations. This enables more complex information pathways, but it also creates greater challenges to the effective management of information. Related to this trend is the rapidly increased extent to which information users are becoming information producers. The World Wide Web presents the most compelling evidence of this; when barriers are reduced sufficiently, greater numbers of people will make information available on the network. When electronic commerce technologies become widely used, in the relatively near future, this will create a rich and complex marketplace for information products.

Integration and Location

National-scale applications involve large numbers of participating organizations with multiple focal points of organizational control and multiple needs for information. They often involve solving information management problems that rely on multiple sources of data, possibly including legacy databases that are difficult to reengineer. This creates a problem of information integration in which multiple information resources, with different schemas, data representations, access management schemes, locations, and other characteristics, may have to be combined to solve queries. As discussed in Chapter 1, sometimes this information can be preassembled and integrated in response to mutually agreed-upon, anticipated needs; however, this is not always feasible. Strategies that make integration feasible are needed to meet the short-term press of crises, and they may well have utility in reducing costs and otherwise facilitating information integration in other, less time-sensitive applications, which Chapter 1 discusses with respect to digital libraries.

Information integration is an area of active research aimed at introducing advances over traditional concepts of wrappers and mediators. A "wrapper" for a database provides it with a new virtual interface, enabling the database to appear to have a particular data model that conforms to a user's requirement for which the database may not have been designed. A "mediator" provides a common presentation for a schema element that is managed differently in a set of related database. A mediator can thus translate different users' requests into the common presentation, which multiple wrappers sharing that presentation can then translate into forms understood by the resources they interact with (i.e., "wrap"). Thus, mediators and wrappers give users a uniform way to access a set of databases integrated into a system, so that they appear as a single virtual aggregate database. In the past, much of this work has been performed on a laborious, ad hoc basis; more general-purpose approaches, such as The Stanford-IBM Manager of Multiple Information Sources (TSIMMIS; see Box 2.4) aim at producing mediation architectures of more general use.

Most research now under way focuses on how a virtual aggregate database can be engineered for a set of existing databases. This involves developing data models and schemas suitable for the virtual aggregate, and mappings among the models and schemas for the component databases and the common data model and schema elements. When this is to be done on more than an ad hoc basis, methods are needed to represent the aggregate schemas. When legacy databases are involved, reverse engineering of those databases may be necessary to determine their schemas. This can be risky, because there are often hidden assumptions and invariants that must be respected if a legacy database is to remain useful. As Yigal Arens, of the University of Southern California, discussed, the information integration problem becomes more difficult when queries to the aggregate database need to be carried out efficiently (subject to a time constraint), creating research challenges for query optimization at the aggregate level.

New approaches in research on information integration are beginning to yield results, but scaling up to national or global scale will significantly complicate the information integration problem. For example, when multiple organizations are involved, access control issues become more important and also more difficult. Just as new schemas are required for the aggregate to reconcile multiple schemas, aggregate access control and security models may also have to be developed. Also, information integration may be complicated by distributed computing issues—for example, a set of databases may be interconnected intermittently or over a low-capacity link, which would affect the way query processing is carried out. This is a familiar issue in distributed databases that becomes more difficult in a heterogeneous setting.

Richer data models have been developed for specialized uses, such as object databases for design applications or information retrieval databases for digital libraries. When these kinds of information assets must be integrated with more traditional databases, the information integration problem can become much more complicated. One way to address this problem is to develop common reusable wrapper and mediator elements that can be adapted easily to apply in a wide range of circumstances.

Applications such as crisis management increase the difficulty of information integration by introducing the need to integrate rapidly a set of databases whose integration was previously not contemplated. The accounts of information management in crisis situations that were presented in the workshops focused on ad hoc information integration solutions designed to meet very specific needs. For example, geographic databases, land use and utility databases, real estate tax databases, and other databases from a variety of sources are necessary to gather information to rapidly process damage claims related to natural disasters such as storms and earthquakes. This suggests that there is value in anticipating this kind of integration, and developing, in advance, a repertoire of task-specific common schemas and associated mediators for legacy databases. This hybrid approach to integration has appeal, in that it supports incremental progress toward common schemas when they can be agreed-upon, and when common schemas cannot be arrived at, mediators can be developed to support interoperability. This also suggests that information integration provides techniques that may be applicable to more general (and less approachable) information fusion problems.[11]

In addition to integration, there is the related issue of information location. Searching within a database of a specific digital library depends upon finding the appropriate database or digital library. As Eliot Christian, of the U.S. Geological Survey, observed:

> **BOX 2.4 INFORMATION INTEGRATION TECHNOLOGIES**
>
> Wrappers and mediators are not new technologies; they have been implemented in an ad hoc fashion for many years. One of the original motivations for work on wrappers was the desire to make legacy programs and information sources (such as databases) accessible to diverse requesting applications across networks. This required laborious, ad hoc production of wrappers that translate requests from users' applications into queries and other commands that the wrapped resources can interpret and will respond to correctly.
>
> Disagreement among workshop participants and additional inputs solicited for this report illustrate the perhaps inevitable breadth of perspectives about what does or does not constitute a new research idea. Some contributors were pessimistic about the likelihood of solving complex integration problems through wrappers and mediators. They suggested, for example, that years of experience have shown that for integration to work well, applications must be written in the expectation that their output will be used as another application's input, or vice versa—leaving unaddressed the problem of integrating legacy programs and information sources that were not written with reuse in mind.[1] Others accepted the truth of this observation, but interpreted it as an opportunity for fundamental research, pointing to recent research aimed at developing architectures within which generic techniques may be found for more rapidly and reliably building software components to integrate diverse resources, including legacy resources. Gio Wiederhold has described one example in this vein, a three-layer mediation architecture consisting of the basic information sources and their wrappers; a mediation layer that adds value by merging, indexing, abstracting, etc.; and the users and their applications that need the information (Wiederhold, 1992).
>
> There is a range of research challenges to make such an architecture broadly useful. For example, models for representing diverse information sources and languages for interacting with them must accommodate not only sources with a well-defined schema (e.g., the relational model used in many databases), but others such as text files, spreadsheets, and multimedia.[2] Automatic or semiautomatic

One of the fundamental issues in information discovery is that one cannot afford to digest all available information and so must rely on abstractions. Yet, the user of information may be working in a context quite different from what the information provider anticipated. While cataloging techniques can characterize a bibliographic information resource statically, I would like to see a "feature extraction" approach that would support abstraction of information resources based more closely on the user's needs at the moment of searching. Natural language processing may help in the direction of search based on knowledge representations, but the more general problem is to support a full range of pattern matching to include imagery and numeric models as well as human language. . . .

generation of wrappers would be a significant contribution; this a serious challenge that requires identifying and representing not only the syntactic interfaces but also the semantic content and assumptions of information sources. Some research has focused on rule-based tools for generating wrappers.

Complementary to research on representing characteristics of sources is the formal representation of domain-specific knowledge that users may need to access and explore. This representation could facilitate generation of mediators optimized for understanding requests and translating them into searches that draw upon and integrate multiple information sources, interacting with each source through a wrapper. Yigal Arens, of the University of Southern California, discussed current research on applying a variety of artificial intelligence techniques to partially automate the creation of mediators for specific applications.[3] In this approach, a model is constructed to describe not only the structure and content of a set of information sources, but also the knowledge domain about which the sources have information. The mediator translates user queries related to that domain into search strategies, which it then implements. Changes in the range of information sources available (e.g., addition of new sources) can be accommodated by changing the domain model, rather than rebuilding the mediator.

---

[1] One contributor noted the similarity between wrappers and Unix pipes. The Unix pipe operator provides a software connection between programs, making the output of one program into the input to another. This allows for plugging together applications in novel ways. Successful integration, however, requires more than just passing inputs and outputs back and forth; the two programs must also share—and therefore might have to have been written with explicit recognition of—a semantic agreement about what those elements mean; otherwise, unpredictable, incorrect results may arise.

[2] The Stanford-IBM Manager of Multiple Information Sources (TSIMMIS) is one approach that offers a data model and a common query language, as well as techniques for generating mediators and networks that integrate multiple mediators. See Garcia-Molina et al., "The TSIMMIS Approach to Mediation: Data Models and Languages (Extended Abstract)," available on line from http://www-db.stanford.edu/tsimmis.

[3] See the SIMS project home page for more information, at http://www.isi.edu/sims.

To me, the most immediate problem is that it is very difficult to find and retrieve information from disparate information sources. Although some progress has been made in building consensus on presentation issues through the likes of Web browsers, tools for client-based network search are conspicuously absent. With server-based searching, one can only search for information in fairly narrow and pre-determined domains, and then only with the particular user interface that the information source thought to provide.

For critical national-scale applications, approaches to this information resource location problem must go beyond the opportunistic searching and browsing characteristic of the Internet. Even when information resources are diverse, if they may have to be used in critical applications—particularly those with urgent deadlines—there would be benefit from registering them and their characteristics in an organized manner. With improvements, for example, in schema description techniques, this could make the information integration problem more approachable as well.

Information location also relates to the distributed computing issues raised above, since one approach involves dispatching not just passive queries to information sources, but active information "agents" that monitor and interact with information stores on an ongoing basis. Information agents may also deploy other information agents, increasing the challenges (both to the initial dispatcher of the agents and to the various willing hosts) of monitoring and managing large numbers of deployed agents.

Meta-Data and Types

Information is becoming more complex, is interpreted to a greater extent, and supports a much wider range of issues. Evidence of the increase in complexity is found in (1) the growing demand for enriched data models, such as enhancements to the relational model for objects and types; (2) the adoption of various schemes for network-based sharing and integration of objects, such as CORBA; (3) the development of databases that more fully interpret objects, such as deductive databases; (4) the rapid growth in commercial standards and repository technology for structured and multimedia objects; and (5) the integration of small software components, such as applets, into structured documents.

One important approach to managing this increased complexity is the use of explicit meta-data and type information. William Arms, of the Corporation for National Research Initiatives, observed, "Very simple, basic information about information is, first of all, a wonderfully important building block and [second,] . . . a much more difficult question than anybody really likes to admit."

Multimedia databases, for example, typically maintain separate stores for the encoded multimedia material and the supporting meta-data. Meta-data provide additional information about an object, beyond the content that is the object itself. Any attribute can be managed as meta-data. For example, in a multimedia database, meta-data could include index tags, information about the beginnings and endings of scenes, and so on. Meta-data can also include quality information. In crisis management applications, this is crucial, since there are some cases where many of the raw data (40 percent, in David Kehrlein's commercial GIS example discussed in Chapter 1) are inaccurate in some respect. As David Austin, of Edgewater, Maryland, noted, "Often, data are merged and summarized to such an extent that differences attributable to sources of varying validity are lost." Separately distinguishable meta-data about the reliability of sources can help users identify and manage around poor-quality data.

Types are a kind of meta-data that provide information on how objects can be interpreted. In this regard, type information is like the more usual database schema. Types, however, can be task specific and ad hoc. Task specificity means, for example, that the particular consensus types in the Multi-purpose Internet Mail Extension (MIME) hierarchy are a small subset of the types that could be developed for a particular application.

Because of this task specificity, the evolution of types presents major challenges. For example, the type a user may adopt for a structured document typically evolves over a period of months or years as a result of migration from one desktop publishing system to the next. Either the user resists migration and falls behind technology developments, or the user must somehow manage a set of objects with similar, but not identical types. One approach to this problem is to create a separate set of servers for types that serve up type information and related capabilities (e.g., conversion mechanisms that allow objects to be transformed from one type to another).

A related issue is the evolution of structured objects to contain software components. The distinction between structured documents and assemblies of software components has been blurring for some time, and this trend will complicate further the effective management of structured objects. For example, because a structured object can contain computation, it is no longer benign from the standpoint of security. An information object could threaten confidentiality by embodying a communications channel back to another host, or it could threaten integrity or service access due to computations it makes while within a protected environment. Many concepts are being developed to address these problems, but their interplay with broader information management issues remains to be worked out. This issue also reinforces the increasing convergence between concepts of information management and concepts of software and computation.

Production and Value

National-scale applications provide many more opportunities for information producers to participate in an increasingly rich and complex information marketplace. Every educator, health care professional, and crisis management decision maker creates information, and that information has a particular audience. Technology to support the efficient production of information and, more generally, the creation of value in an information value chain is becoming increasingly important in many application areas and on the Internet in general.

The World Wide Web, even in its present early state of development, provides evidence of the wide range of kinds of value that can be provided beyond what are normally thought of as original content. For example, among the most popular Web services are sites that catalog and index other sites. Many sites are popular because they assess and evaluate other sites. There are services emerging for brokering of information, either locating sites in response to queries or locating likely consumers of produced specialty information. Because of the speed of the electronic network, many steps can be made very efficiently along the way from initial producer to end consumer of information.

Related to these concepts of information value are new information services. For example, there are several candidate services that support commerce in information objects. Because information objects can be delivered rapidly and reliably, they can support commerce models that are very different from models for physical objects. In addition, services are emerging to support information retrieval, serving of complex multimedia objects, and the like. The profusion of information producers on the Web also creates a need for a technology that enables successful small-scale services to scale up to larger-scale and possibly institutional-level services. National-scale applications such as crisis management complicate this picture because they demand attention to quality and timeliness. Thus the capability of an information retrieval system, for example, may be measured in terms of functions ranging from resource availability (for meeting a deadline) to precision and recall.

Distribution and Relocation

As noted above, distributed information resources may have to be applied, in the aggregate, to support national-scale applications. In these applications, there can be considerable diversity that must be managed. The distributed information resources can be public or private, with varying access control, security, and payment provisions. They can include traditional databases, wide-area file systems, digital libraries, object databases, multimedia databases, and miscellaneous ad hoc information resources. They can be available on a major network, on storage media, or in some other form. They also can include a broad range of kinds of data, such as structured text, images, audio, video, multimedia, and application-specific structured types.

For many applications, these issues can interact in numerous ways. For example, when network links are of low capacity or are intermittent, in many cases it may be acceptable to degrade quality. Alternatively, relative availability, distribution, and quality of communications and computing resources may determine the extent to which data and computation migrate over the distributed network. For example, low-capacity links and limited computing resources at the user's location may suggest that query processing is best done at the server; but when clients have significant computing resources and network capacity is adequate, then query processing, if it is complex, could be done at the client site. When multiple distributed databases cooperate in responding to queries, producing aggregated responses, this resource-balancing problem can become more complex; when atomicity and replication issues are taken into account, it can become even more difficult.

In crisis management, resource management and availability issues take on new dimensions. In a crisis, complex information integration problems may yield results that go into public information kiosks. When communications are intermittent or resource constrained, caching and replication techniques must respond to levels of demand that are unanticipated or are changing rapidly. Can data replicate and migrate effectively without direct manual guidance and intervention? This is more difficult when there are data quality problems or when kiosks support direct interaction and creation of new information.

USER-CENTERED SYSTEMS: DESIGNING APPLICATIONS TO WORK WITH PEOPLE

Research on natural, intuitive user interface technologies has been under way for many years. Although significant progress has been made, workshop participants indicated that a more comprehensive view of the human-computer interface as part of larger systems must be developed in order for these technologies to yield the greatest benefit. Allen Sears observed, "The fact that humans make . . . errors, the fact that humans are impatient, the fact that humans forget—these are the kinds of issues that we need to deal with in integrating humans into the process. The flip side of that . . . is that humans, compared to computers, have orders-of-magnitude more domain-specific knowledge, general knowledge, common sense, and ability to deal with uncertainty."

System designs should focus on integrating humans into the system, not just on providing convenient human-computer interfaces. The term "system" today commonly refers to the distributed, heterogeneous networks, computers, and information that users interact with to build and run applications and to accomplish other tasks. A more useful and accurate view of the user-system relationship is of users as an integral part of the total system and solution space. Among other advantages, this view highlights the need for research integrating computing and communications science and engineering with advances in the understanding of user and organizational characteristics from the social sciences.

Human-centered Systems and Interfaces

Traditional human-computer interface research embraces a wide array of technologies, such as speech synthesis, visualization and virtual reality, recognition of multiple input modes (e.g., speech, gesture, handwriting), language understanding, and many others.[12] All applications can benefit from easy and natural interfaces, but these are relative characteristics that vary for different users and settings. A basic principle is that the presentation should be as natural to use as possible, to minimize demands on those with no time or attention to spare for learning how to use an application. This does not necessarily imply simplicity; an interface that is too simple may not provide some capabilities the user needs and lead to frustration.

In addition, designers of interfaces in large-scale applications with diverse users cannot depend on the presence of a particular set of computing and communications resources, so the interfaces must be adaptable to what is available. The network-distributed nature of many applications requires attention to the scaling of user interfaces across a range of available platforms, with constraints that are diverse and—especially in crises—unpredictable. Constraints include power consumption in portable computers and communications bandwidth. For example, it is important that user interfaces and similar services for accessing a remote computing resource be usable, given the fidelity and quality of service available to the user. An additional focus for research in making interface technologies usable in national-scale applications is reducing their cost.

Crisis management, however, highlights the need to adapt not only to available hardware and software, but also to the user. Variations in training and skills affect what users can do with applications and how they can best interact with them. As David Austin observed:

> Training is also critical; people with the proper skill mix are often in short supply. We have not leveraged the technology sufficiently to deliver short bursts of training to help a person gain sufficient proficiency to perform the task of the moment. . . .
> [What is needed is] a system that optimizes both the human element and the information technology element using ideas from the object technology world. In such a system, a person's skills would be considered an object; as the person gained and lost skill proficiency over his career, he would be trained and given different jobs [so that he could be part of] a high-performance work force able to match any in the world. The approach involves matching a person with a job and at the same time understanding the skill shortfalls, training in short bursts, and/or tutoring to obtain greater proficiency. As shortfalls are understood by the person, he or she can task the infrastructure to provide just-in-time, just-enough training at the time and place the learner wants and needs it.

In addition, because conditions such as stress and information overload can vary rapidly during a crisis, there would also be value in an ability to monitor the user's performance (e.g., through changes in response time or dexterity) and adapt in real time to the changing capabilities of users under stress. By using this information, applications such as a "crisis manager's electronic aide" could adjust filtering and prioritization to reduce the flood of information given to the user. Improvements in techniques for data fusion in real time among sensors and other inputs would enhance the quality of this filtering. Applications could also be designed to alter their presentation to provide assistance, such as warnings, reminders, or step-by-step menus, if the user appears to be making increasing numbers of errors.

The focus of these opportunities is inherently multidisciplinary. To achieve significant advances in the usability of applications, improvements in particular interface techniques can be augmented by integrating multiple, complementary technologies. Recent research in multimodal interfaces has proceeded from the recognition that no single technique is always the best for even a single user, much less for all users, all the time, and that a combination of techniques can be more effective than any single one. Learning how to optimize the interface mode for any given situation requires experimentation, as well as building on social science research in areas such as human factors and organizational behavior.

Recognizing that the ideal for presentation of information to the user is in a form and context that is understandable, workshop participants noted that in some applications a visual presentation is called for. Given adequate performance, an immersive virtual reality environment could benefit applications such as crisis management training, telemedicine, and manufacturing design. In crisis management training especially, a realistic recreation of operational conditions (such as the appearance of damaged structures, the noise and smoke of fires and storms, the sound of explosions) can help reproduce—and therefore train for—the stress-inducing sensations that prevail in the field. Because response to a crisis is inherently a collaborative activity, simulations should synthesize a single, consistent, evolving situation that can be observed from many distinct points of view by the team members.[13]

Don Eddington identified a common perception of the crisis situation as a feature that is essential to effective collaboration. A depiction of the geographic neighborhood of a crisis can provide an organizing frame of reference. Photographs and locations of important or damaged facilities, visual renderings of simulation results, logs of team activity, locations of other team members, notes—all can attach to points on a map. Given adequate bandwidth and computing capacity, another way to provide this common perception might be through synthetic virtual environments, displaying a visualization of the situation that could be shared among many crisis managers. (The Crisis 2005 scenario presented in Box 1.3 suggests a long-range goal for implementing this concept such that a crisis manager could be projected into a virtual world optimized to represent the problem at hand in a way that enhances the user's intuition.) Research challenges underlying such visualizations include ways to integrate and display information from diverse sources, including real observations (e.g., from field reports or sensors) and simulations. The variation in performance among both equipment and skills of different users may prevent displaying precisely the same information to all users; presumably, some minimal common elements are necessary to enable collaboration. Determining precisely what information and display features should be common to all collaborators is an example of the need for technology design to be complemented with multidisciplinary research in areas such as cognition and organizational behavior.

Collaboration and Virtual Organizations

Because people work in groups, collaboration support that helps them communicate and share information and resources can be of great benefit. Crisis management has a particularly challenging need: an instant bureaucracy to respond effectively to a crisis. In a crisis, there is little prior knowledge of who will be involved or what resources will be available; nevertheless, a way must be found to enable them to work together to get their jobs done. This implies assembling resources and groups of people into organized systems that no one could know ahead of time would have to work together. Multiple existing bureaucracies, infrastructures, and individuals must be assembled and formed into an effective virtual organization. The instant bureaucracy of a crisis response organization is an even more unpredictable, horizontal, and heterogeneous structure than is implied by traditional command and control models of military organizations in warfare—themselves a complex collaboration challenge. Crisis management collaboration must accommodate this sort of team building rapidly; thus, it provides requirements for developing and opportunities for testing collaboration technologies that are rapidly configurable and support complex interactions.

One relatively near-term opportunity is to develop and use the concept of anchor desks (discussed above, in the section "Distributed Computing"). The concept has been tested in technology demonstrations such as JWID (see Chapter 1); field deployment in civilian crises could be used to stress the underlying concepts and identify research needs. Anchor desks can provide a resource for efficient, collaborative use of information, particularly where multiple organizations must be coordinated. They represent a hybrid between decentralized and centralized information management. Each anchor desk could support a particular functional need, such as logistics or weather forecasting. A crisis management anchor desk would presumably be located outside the crisis zone, for readier access to worldwide information sources and expertise; however, it would require sufficient communication with people working at the scene of the crisis to be useful to them, as well as the ability to deliver information in scalable forms appropriate to the recipient's available storage and display capabilities (e.g., a geographic information system data file representing the disaster scene for one, a static map image for another, a text file for a third).

An anchor desk could not only integrate data from multiple sources, but also link it with planning aides, such as optimized allocation of beds and medicines and prediction of optimal evacuation routes implemented as electronic overlays on geographic information systems, with tools involving a range of artificial intelligence, information retrieval, integration, and simulation technologies. An anchor desk could also house a concentration of information analysts and subject matter experts (e.g., chemists, as envisioned in the Crisis 2005 scenario); computing resources for modeling, simulation, data fusion, and decision support; information repositories; and others.

Anchor desks could provide services to support cross-organizational collaboration, such as tools for rapidly translating data files, images, and perhaps even human languages into forms usable by different groups of people. Furthermore, the anchor desk might not be physically at one place; a logically combined, but physically separated, collection of networked resources could perform the same function, opening the possibility for multiple ways of incorporating the capability into the architecture of the crisis response organization. The set of technologies implied by this sort of anchor desk could serve to push research not only in each technology, but also in tools and architectures for integrating these capabilities, such as whiteboards and video-conferencing systems that scale for different users' capacities and can correctly integrate multiple security levels in one system.

Nevertheless, information must be integrated not only at remote locations such as command centers and anchor desks, but also at field sites. David Kehrlein, of the Office of Emergency Services, State of California, noted, "Solutions require development of on-site information systems and an integration of those with the central systems. If you don't have on-site intelligence, you don't know a lot."

Judgment Support

The most powerful component of any system for making decisions in a crisis is a person with knowledge and training. However, crisis decision making is marked by underuse of information and overreliance on personal expertise in an environment that is turbulent and rich in information flows. The expert, under conditions of information overload, acts as if he or she has no information at all. Providing access to information is not enough. The ability to evaluate, filter, and integrate information is the key to its being used.

Filtering and integrating could be done separately for each person on that person's individual workstation. However, a more useful approach for any collaborative activity would be to integrate and allocate information within groups of users. (In fact, information filtering at the boundary of a linked group of users could be one of the most important services performed by the virtual subnets discussed above in the section "Networking"; filters could help individuals and groups avoid information-poor decision making in an information-rich environment.) Information integration techniques such as those discussed in the section "Information Management" are generally presented in terms of finding the best information from diverse sources to meet the user's needs. The flip side of this coin is the advantage of being able to cull the second-best and third-best information, reducing the unmanageable flood.

A set of special needs of crisis management, which may have significant utility in other application areas as well, can be captured in the concept of judgment support. A crisis manager often makes intuitive judgments in real time that correspond to previously undefined problems without complete contingency plans. This should be contrasted with traditional notions of decision support, which are associated with a more methodical, rule-based approach to previously defined and studied problems. Judgment support for crisis management could rely on rule-based expert systems to some extent, but the previously defined problems used to train these systems will necessarily be somewhat different from any given crisis. Workshop participants suggested a need for automated support comparing current situations with known past cases. To achieve this automation, however, much better techniques are required for abstractly representing problems, possible solutions, and the sensitivity of predicted outcomes to variations, gaps, and uncertain quality in available information.

The last point is particularly important for crises, because it is inevitable that some of the information the judgment maker relies upon will be of low quality. Two examples are the poor quality of maps that crisis management experts remarked on in the workshops and the rapid rate of change in some crises that continually renders knowledge about the situation obsolete. The technology for representing problem spaces and running computations on them must therefore be able to account for the degree of uncertainty about information. Moreover, data may not always vary in a statistically predictable way (e.g., Gaussian distribution). In some kinds of crises, data points may be skewed unpredictably by an active adversary (e.g., a terrorist or criminal), by someone attempting to hide negligence after an accident, or by unexpected failure modes in a sensor network.

Another reason the challenge of representing problems may be particularly difficult in crisis management is that the judgments needed are often multidimensional in ways that are inherently difficult to represent. James Beauchamp's call for tools to help optimize not only the operational and logistical dimensions of a foreign disaster relief operation, but also the political consequences of various courses of action, illustrates the complexity of the problem. Even presenting the variables in a way that represents and could allow balancing among all dimensions of the problem is not possible with current techniques. By contrast, the multidimensional problem discussed in Chapter 1 (see the section "Manufacturing")—simulating and optimizing trade-offs among such facets as product performance parameters, material costs, manufacturability, and full product life-cycle costs—although extremely complex computationally, is perhaps more feasible to define in terms with which computer models can work.

If a problem can be represented adequately, a judgment support system should be able to assist the judgment maker by giving context and consequences from a multidimensional exploration of the undefined problem represented by the current crisis. This context construction requires automated detection and classification of issues and anomalies, identifying outlier data points (which could represent errors, but could also indicate emerging new developments), and recognizing relationships between the current situation and previously known cases that may have been missed by or unknown to the crisis manager.

Because judgments are ultimately made by people, not computers, technologies intended to support making judgments must be designed for ease of use and with an ability to understand and take into account the capabilities and needs of the user. To a great extent, of course, it is up to the user to ask for the information he or she needs, but a model of what knowledge that individual already has could be used to alter the system's information integration and presentation approaches dynamically. Another special application for crisis management is monitoring the decision maker, because of the stress and fatigue factors that come into play. Performance monitors could detect when the user's performance is slipping, by detecting slowed reaction time and onset of errors. This information could guide a dynamic alteration in the degree of information filtering, along with variations in the user interface (such as simpler menu options). These capabilities could be of more general value. For example, they could assist in assessing the effectiveness of multimedia training and education tools in schools and continuing-education applications.

Of course, to be useful, a monitoring capability would have to be integrated properly with the way users actually use systems. For example, users will ignore a system that instructs them to get some rest when rest is not an option. Instead, it might be valuable for a system to switch to a standard operating procedures-oriented, step-by-step interface when the user shows signs of tiring. Human factors research provides useful insights, including some that are of generic usefulness. However, needs will always vary with the context of specific applications, implying the strong necessity for researchers and application users to interact during testing and deployment of systems and design of new research programs (Drabek, 1991).

NOTES

1. Partridge, Craig, and Frank Kastenholz, "Technical Criteria for Choosing IP the Next Generation (IPng)," Internet Request for Comments 1726, December 1994. Available on line from http://www.cis.ohio-state.edu/hypertext/information/rfc.html.

2. Services and technologies are now emerging that may meet this need, such as cellular digital packet data and digital spread-spectrum. Portable terminals that can be used to communicate via satellite uplink are an additional exception; however, such systems are not yet portable or affordable enough that many relief workers in a crisis could carry one for general use.

3. Noncommercial, amateur packet radio is a counterexample; however, commercial service offerings are lacking. Part of the problem is the lack of methods of accounting for use of the spectrum in peer-to-peer packet radio networks, without which there is a potential problem of overuse of the spectrum—a tragedy of the commons.

4. A description of the proposed demonstration is available on line at the JWID '96 home page, http://www.spawar.navy.mil.

5. Many telephone carriers now provide frame-relay virtual subnets that are intended to support the isolation discussed here. One serious drawback at present is that their establishment is on a custom basis and is both labor intensive and time-consuming. Telephone carriers are likely to adopt a more automated order fulfillment process as demand grows, but it remains technically infeasible to requisition and establish these services in the heat of a crisis to solve an immediate problem.

6. Given the current costliness of access to high-performance computation and high-speed network services, achieving this gain will require political and economic decisions about making resources available, perhaps based on building a case that this investment could yield a positive payoff by lowering the eventual cost of responding to crises.

7. In addition, the coarser-grained simulation can be used to provide dynamically consistent

boundary conditions around the areas examined in finer detail. The model, called the Advanced Regional Prediction System, is written in Fortran and designed for scalability. See Droegemeier (1993) and Xue et al. (1996). See also "The Advanced Regional Prediction System," available on line at http://wwwcaps.uoknor.edu/ARPS.

8. A CAPS technical paper explains that "although no meteorological prediction or simulation codes we know of today were designed with massive parallelism in mind, we believe it is now possible to construct models that take full advantage of such architecture." See "The Advanced Regional Prediction System: Model Design Philosophy and Rationale," available on line at http://wwwcaps.uoknor.edu/ARPS.

9. The ability to effectively handle time as a resource is an issue not only for integrating real-time data, but for distributed computing systems in general. Formal representation of temporal events and temporal constraints, and scheduling and monitoring distributed computing processes with hard real-time requirements, are fundamental research challenges. Some research progress has been made in verifying limited classes of real-time computable applications and implementing prototype distributed real-time operating systems.

10. Details about I-WAY are available on line at http://www.iway.org.

11. One key data fusion challenge involves data alignment and registration, where data from different sources are aligned to different norms.

12. Some key challenges underlying communication between people and machines relate to information representation and understanding. These are addressed primarily in the section, "Information Management," but it should be understood that without semantic understanding of, for example, a user's requests, no interface technology will produce a good result.

13. This concept is currently used for military training in instances when high-performance computation is available; trainees' computers are linked to the high-performance systems that generate the simulation, and the trainees see a more or less realistic virtual crisis (OTA, 1995). Nonmilitary access to such simulations likely requires lower-cost computing resources.

3

Summary and Findings: Research for National-scale Applications

RESEARCH CHALLENGES OF CRISIS MANAGEMENT

Crises can make enormous demands on the widely distributed information resources of a nation (see summary in Box 3.1). Responding to the Oklahoma City bombing disaster required a national call for search and rescue experts and their tools to help find survivors and to reinforce unstable areas of the damaged Alfred P. Murrah Building so that rescuers could enter safely, as well as massive coordination to focus a diverse set of teams on a common goal. Hurricane Andrew and the Northridge, California, earthquake caused widespread devastation and placed pressure on relief authorities to distribute food, water, shelter, and medicine and to begin receiving and approving applications for disaster assistance without delay.

Crises often bring together many different organizations that do not normally work together, and these groups may require resources that they have not used before. To mount an organized response in this environment, crisis managers can benefit from the use of information technology to catalog, coordinate, analyze, and predict needs; to report status; and to track progress. This kind of coordinated management requires communications networks, from handheld radios and the public telephone network to high-speed digital networks for voice, video, and data. Rapidly deployable communications technologies can help relief teams communicate and coordinate their actions and pool their resources. Crisis managers also need computers to help them retrieve, organize, process, and share information, and they rely on computer models to help them analyze and predict complex phenomena such as weather and damage to buildings or other structures.

> **BOX 3.1 SUMMARY OF CRISIS MANAGEMENT CHARACTERISTICS AND NEEDS**
>
> 1. Crises make large-scale demands, are unpredictable, and require an immediate response.
> - Large-scale demands. Crises require resources beyond those on hand—people, equipment, communications, information, and computing must be moved rapidly to the scene physically and/or virtually (over networks).
> - Unpredictable. It cannot be known in advance what resources will be needed or where, and what the specific needs will be (although there can be some degree of generalizing and pre-positioning).
> - Urgent. The response must be rapid, because lives and property are at stake.
> 2. Crises require planning and coordination.
> - Crisis managers must develop and implement a response plan rapidly, despite information shortfalls (gaps, uncertainty, errors, deliberate falsification by a foe) and the lack of correspondence to any previous situations (i.e., standard operating procedures are not sufficient).
> - Diverse organizations and people respond to crises, including those that have not worked together before and did not know that they would have to do so. This creates challenges for collaboration, information sharing, and communication.
> - Crises are complex and multifaceted, and so decision makers must weigh multifaceted consequences. Trade-offs require not just tactical optimization, but judgment—the best tactical option may not be the best political option (e.g., in an international context where U.S. military and civilian agencies are operating in another country, perhaps in a tense situation).
> 3. Operational needs include communications and networking.
> - A rapid initial assessment of the situation is necessary, requiring reports from the scene, augmented by sending assessment teams with tools and communications to report back quickly. Remote sensing may also be involved (e.g., satellite and aircraft imagery, ground-based weather monitors, and strain gauges predeployed within bridges and buildings).

When disasters occur, the public deserves and demands a rapid response, and so the ability to anticipate events is at a premium. For example, when a hurricane approaches, relief agencies deploy mobile communications centers to places where sophisticated computer models predict the storm will strike land. Damage simulations help planners decide where to send food, medicine, shelters, blankets, and other basic necessities even before the damage has occurred. As the response to California's Northridge earthquake demonstrated, relief agencies can use computer simulation to speed the approval of disaster relief (e.g., home rebuilding loans) in areas that the model estimates are hard hit, even before agents have visited the site.

- Rapid deployment of communications capabilities is required—to expand the initial situation assessment, coordinate the response teams, and disseminate information to the public. It is necessary to (a) assess what is available (remote regions, less developed countries, and badly damaged areas may all have limited infrastructure) and (b) obtain needed capabilities by commandeering what is there (priority access), restoring networks, and augmenting with deployable capabilities (cellular telephones, wireless networks, sensors) as needed.
- Required communications parameters must be defined and implemented rapidly. These include (a) reliability (crucial for life-critical communications, e.g., fire and rescue, telemedicine); and (b) security—to maintain confidentiality (especially if an active adversary is involved, but also to protect any private information that is communicated), maintain the integrity of information, and authenticate certain users to allow them priority access.
- Crises require more than voice communications—text, all types of sensor outputs, images, full-motion video, and data files must also be communicated; all involve different technological requirements and trade-offs (e.g., latency, quality, bandwidth).
- Crises demand integration across a wide, unpredictable scale of resources; thus, there must be flexibility about centralization versus distribution: (a) computing and communications that are available at or accessible to the crisis team include laptops and wireless at the scene, workstations and T-1 (1.5 megabits per second) data links at the command center, and fully distributed computing and communications (e.g., World Wide Web, remote supercomputers) outside the crisis zone; (b) flows of information throughout (into, out of, within) this architecture are unpredictable and may change during the crisis itself.
- At the scene, computers and communications platforms must be mobile and untethered.
  4. Operational needs also include information resources and computation.
- There is a need for multifaceted information—multiple modes (voice, video, images, text, sensors, geographic information system (GIS) data, relational databases, and so on).
- It cannot be predicted in advance which multiple sources will be required. Sources (a) cannot be used if crisis managers cannot find them or do not know about them (discovery); (b) cannot be used unless they can be accessed and

Preparing for and responding to crises place demands on information technology that cannot be satisfied readily with existing tools, products, and services. These unmet demands point to many promising research directions, which this chapter summarizes. They encompass most aspects of computing and communications technology, including networks and the architectures and conventions that organize and manage them; the services and standards that unite a network of communications devices, sensors, computers, and databases into a useful information infrastructure; and the applications that rely on that infrastructure.

> - integrated into a crisis manager's information system (interoperability, composability, access rights—intellectual property, privacy); and (c) cannot be used if the crisis managers are flooded with information. Some kind of automated help is needed to sort information—not just filtering it, but also integrating the information to reduce the flow and detecting patterns that can help with interpretation.
> - Information systems must continually check and integrate new information coming in from the field.
> - There is a real-time demand: for example, simulation or model data (e.g., weather forecast) will not be useful if they arrive late.
> 5. Crisis management in a broader context involves other needs as well.
> - Crisis management draws on other application domains, for example: (a) secure electronic commerce for locating, purchasing, and distributing relief supplies and services; (b) digital libraries as means for information discovery, integration, and presentation for crisis managers; (c) secure telemedicine and distributed medical records to facilitate the delivery of emergency care in the field; and (d) manufacturing and distributed design, which, although not applicable in real time (during a crisis), reflect common interests such as distributed modeling, simulation, shared databases, and virtual environments for collaboration.
> - Application needs for technology exist in a broader context as well: (a) solving crisis management problems is not just a computing or communications issue, given that it also involves political, managerial, social, and educational issues; (b) the political, economic, and marketplace context affects the availability of technology resources (hardware, software, information) for crisis management—thus, affordability is essential; and (c) the sociology of organizations affects how they use these technologies.
> - Complex systems must be tested in operational contexts to validate research and determine new research needs.
>
> NOTE: See Chapter 1 for a detailed discussion of the crisis management characteristics and needs that create demands for computing and communications.

One common thread among the steering committee's findings is that some of the most severe technical challenges stem from the sheer scale of requirements that must be met. Scale in this context has many dimensions—the large number of people and devices (e.g., computers, databases, sensors) involved; the diversity of information resources and software applications that must be accessible; the amount of computing power needed to run models and process information quickly enough to meet the urgent demands of crises, along with the ability to access and use that power rapidly and easily; and the complexity of the interactions among systems (both human and technical) that must interwork to deal with crises.

Another theme is that technologies must be easy enough to use that they complement people, rather than distract them from their mission. Technology does nothing by itself; people use technology, and designers and developers of technical systems must consider people and their methods of working as integral to the systems and their successful performance. For example, a secure, distributed information system may fail to remain secure in practice if it is so cumbersome that users ignore necessary procedures in favor of convenience. Too often, unfortunately, users are given too little consideration in the design of complex systems, and the systems consequently fail to be as useful as they could or should be. In the extreme case of a crisis, a system that is difficult to use will not be used at all.

Research on and development of computing and communications technologies that help crisis managers cope with extreme time pressures and the unpredictability of crises will likely be useful in other application areas domains.[1] For example, breakthroughs in meeting the time-critical information discovery and integration requirements of crisis management would benefit broader digital library applications as well. Distributed simulation and the need to compose existing, legacy information sources and software smoothly into new, case-specific systems are among the overlaps with manufacturing. Secure, mobile communication in a crisis is also valuable for emergency medicine, particularly as confidential medical records begin to be communicated over networks. Tools that are easy to use in a crisis will probably also be usable for electronic commerce, which similarly must span a wide range of personal skills, computer platforms, and network access mechanisms.

Although many of the research issues identified throughout the workshop series are not new to the computing and communications research community, placing them in the context of crisis management and other national-scale applications suggests priorities and sharpens the research focus. The priorities fall across a spectrum. Research projects tied relatively closely to specific crisis management application needs are valuable both because of the potential benefit to the applications and for the advances they may produce in technology usable in other areas. Box 3.2 presents promising examples from the workshops.

To secure the full benefits of this application-specific research, there must also be recognition of the broader, increasingly interconnected context in which national-scale applications operate. These interconnections allow components to be called on in unforeseen ways. This presents powerful opportunities for creative new uses of resources, but only if technical challenges to these novel uses can be overcome. During Hurricane Andrew, for example, it was not only the difficulty of translating between different standards that delayed Dade County authorities from making data available to federal relief officials, but also their

BOX 3.2 SELECTED CRISIS MANAGEMENT APPLICATION-SPECIFIC RESEARCH

The discussions between crisis management experts and technologists at the three Computer Science and Telecommunications Board workshops led to identification of a variety of compelling, application-motivated computer science and engineering research topics. A selection of these topics is presented here. It is not an exhaustive list of the technologies needed to solve problems in crisis management, nor does it imply that technological advances are crisis management's most dire needs. However, these topics do appear promising in terms of advancing the state of technology and testing broader architectural concepts.

1. A self-configuring wireless data network for linking crisis field stations could create a capability that does not exist today for crisis managers to coordinate information. It could produce advances useful in other domains, such as hospital or school networking, and could provide useful tests for new communications protocols and network management methods based on, for example, self-identification by components and resources on networks to other components that call upon them.
2. Adaptive networks could be developed that discover and react to changes in available communications links and changing patterns of traffic. They could, for example, route traffic around points of network failure and take advantage of links that become available after a crisis begins, such as the self-configuring wireless network described above or parts of the public switched telecommunications network. This research could stimulate more general work on adaptivity in communications hardware and network management software in contexts other than crises.
3. In crisis management (as well as in military command and control), there is a need for research on "judgment support" tools that can assist crisis managers in making decisions based on incomplete knowledge of conditions, capabilities, and needs, by drawing on information from diverse and unanticipated sources. Such tools would interpret information about the quality and reliability of varied inputs and assist the user in taking these variations into account. They would differ from, but could build upon, traditional decision support tools such as knowledge-based systems, which operate using rules associated with previously examined problems. Because many of the problems raised by crisis management are not known ahead of time, more general techniques are needed. These might include the development of new representations of the quality of inputs (such as meta-data about those inputs), data fusion, models of information representation and integration, rapidly reconfigurable knowledge-based systems, and new techniques for filtering and presenting information to users.
4. A meta-computer resource would provide rapid allocation of distributed computing resources outside a crisis zone to meet crisis management needs for modeling and simulation. Because crises are intermittent and unpredictable, but require real-time urgent response, this research would highlight ways to bring computers, storage, and communications on line rapidly. It would also require new ways to coordinate resources across infrastructure that was not previously set aside for that purpose.

5. Crisis management can motivate simulation research in hurricane landfall prediction, severe storm prediction, atmospheric dispersion of toxic substances, urban fire spread, and many other modeling and simulation problems. To be useful in actual crisis response, these simulations must be linked with inputs such as environmental sensor data in real time and must be able to produce outputs in readily usable form. They should also support a capability to focus the simulation on specific locations and scales in response to requests from crisis managers. In addition, better simulation of human behavior and social phenomena could provide more realistic training and decision support for crisis managers by indicating consequences of decisions on public opinion, international tensions, financial markets, and other areas.
6. Multimedia fusion of data coming from varied, unexpected sources, including imagery (e.g., still photographs and video from amateur citizens with video cameras, news helicopters, automated teller machine security cameras), sensor data (e.g., weather, seismology, structural stress gauges in bridges and buildings); and information from databases (e.g., locations of buildings and roads from a geographic information system (GIS), names of residents and businesses from telephone directories) will be necessary. The ability to integrate information in response to unanticipated queries could be facilitated by automated tagging of data with relevant meta-data (e.g., source, time, image resolution).
7. There is a need for virtual anchor desks in crisis management, with a mixture of people and machines and adaptive augmentation as necessary. Anchor desks for specific functional or subject areas (e.g., logistics, weather forecasting, handling of toxic substances) would provide a resource of computational power, information, and expertise (both human and machine) to crisis officials. The anchor desk capability could be distributed throughout the nation and assembled on call via networks in response to crises. Research issues related to this effort might include new models of information needs within organizations and optimizing the balance of computation, communications, and storage inside and outside the crisis zone.
8. Adaptive interfaces for crisis managers could respond to changing user performance under stress by observing usage patterns and testing for user errors. Crisis management tools could adapt to the performance of the user—for example, by presenting information more slowly and clearly and, if necessary, warning the user that he or she needs rest. Such tools ideally would operate on platforms across the wide scale of computing and display capabilities (e.g., processing, storage, and bandwidth) available in crisis management.
9. Geographic information systems that are more capable than current ones could integrate many data formats (which would promote competition among information providers) and many types of information (such as pictures and real-time links to sensors). Integration should include registering and incorporating these data types fully into the coordinate representation and relational model of the GIS, not just appending markers to points on maps. The GIS should more naturally display crucial factors that are not currently shown clearly, such as uncertainty of data points. Finally, it should be affordable and usable for field workers with laptop computers.

hesitancy to share private data, which relates to the lack of reliable, in-place mechanisms for ensuring privacy and payment for those data. Therefore, applications require both efforts focused on specific needs and a broadly deployed information infrastructure, including services that help people and their tools to achieve integration, and standards and architectures that provide consistent interactions between elements at all levels.

Information infrastructure, of course, does not spring into existence from a vacuum. The workshops reinforced the observation that in crisis management and other national-scale applications, diversity—of people, organizations, methods of working, and technologies (e.g., databases, computers, software)—impedes creating national architectures from scratch. (See Box S.2 in the chapter "Summary and Overview" for further discussion.) Although it might be possible to imagine a single, uniform architecture that met crisis managers' needs for communications interoperability, data interchange, remote access to computation, and others, deploying it would not be practicable. The technical challenge of incorporating legacy systems into the new architecture would slow such an effort. In addition, many public and private organizations would have to agree to invest in new technologies in concert, but no single architecture could conform to all organizations' needs and work modes. Retraining and reorganizing organizations' processes to accommodate new systems would take time. Finally, crisis management illustrates that even a coherent architecture created for one domain would be called upon to integrate in unexpected ways with other domains.

Therefore, there is a need for—and the steering committee's findings address—research, development, and deployment efforts leading both to consistent architectural approaches that work on national scales and to general-purpose tools and services that make ad hoc integration of existing and new systems and resources easier. Specific applications, such as those listed in Box 3.2, should serve to test these approaches, to advance key technologies, and to meet important application needs. The organization of the findings reflects this view that both application-targeted and broader infrastructural research is needed. Finding 1 emphasizes the importance of experimental testbeds as a context for coordinating the crucial interplay among research, development, and deployment in one important and challenging application area, crisis management. Finding 2 highlights the value of investigating the features of existing national-scale architectures to identify principles underlying their successes and failures. These findings are discussed in the section "Technology Deployment and Research Progress."

The remaining findings identify architectural concerns that represent technological leverage points for computing and communications research investments, the outcomes of which could benefit many national-scale applications. The research underlying these findings is discussed in greater detail in Chapter 2. The findings abstract the common threads among the networking, computation, information, and user-centered technologies of Chapter 2 to indicate high-priority application-motivated research needs that cross multiple levels of computing and communications. There is necessarily some overlap in the research issues discussed in these areas, because some technological approaches can contribute to meeting more than one architectural objective. These findings are presented in four subsequent sections:

- Support of Human Activities
    Finding 3: Usability
    Finding 4: Collaboration
- System Composability and Interoperability
    Finding 5: Focused Standards
    Finding 6: Interoperability
    Finding 7: Integration of Software Components
    Finding 8: Legacy and Longevity
- Adapting to Uncertainty and Change
    Finding 9: Adaptivity
    Finding 10: Reliability
- Performance of Distributed Systems
    Finding 11: Performance of Distributed Systems

Outcomes of testbed and architecture study activities (see Findings 1 and 2) can and should inform future reexamination of findings in these architectural areas, which represent the best understanding of a range of technology and application experts in 1995-1996.

The findings frame research derived primarily from addressing the requirements of crisis management. However, the steering committee believes that such research would have much broader utility, because of the extreme nature of the demands that crises place on technology. In addition, many of the research directions relate to increasing the capabilities of information infrastructure to meet extreme demands for ease of use, integration, flexibility, and distributed performance, which will benefit any application using it. The findings are illustrated by practical needs identified in the workshops and examples of specific directions that researchers could pursue. These suggestions are not intended to be exhaustive, nor are they presented in priority order; deployment and experimentation are required to determine which approaches work best. However, they are promising starting directions, and they illustrate the value of studying applications as a source of research goals.

TECHNOLOGY DEPLOYMENT AND RESEARCH PROGRESS

The workshop series focused on applications partly in the recognition that computing and communications research and development processes depend on the deployment and use of the technology they create. This is true not only in the sense that efficient allocation of research investments should lead ideally to products and services that people want, but also in the sense that it is ultimately through deployment and use that technologists can test the validity of their theories and technical approaches. This is not a unique recognition; it fits within a stream of recent analyses, including a strategic implementation plan of the Committee on Information and Communications, *America in the Age of Information* (CIC, 1995a) and the Computer Science and Telecommunications Board review of the High Performance Computing and Communications Initiative (HPCCI), *Evolving the High Performance Computing and Communications Initiative to Support the Nation's Information Infrastructure* (CSTB, 1995a). The opportunities that the steering committee's first two findings identify for learning from study of deployed technologies, however, have not received extensive attention to date.

BOX 3.3 CRISIS MANAGEMENT TESTBEDS: RELATIONSHIP TO PREVIOUS VISIONS

The Committee on Information and Communications (CIC) has called for "pilot implementations, applications testbeds, and demonstrations, presenting opportunities to test and improve new underlying information and communications technologies, including services for information infrastructures." (CIC, 1995a, p. 8) The CIC plan anticipates these testbeds and demonstrations as fitting into three broad classes of user-driven applications related to long-term National Science and Technology Council goals:

- High-performance applications for science and engineering (modeling and simulation, focused on the Grand Challenges);
- High-confidence applications for dynamic enterprises (security, reliability, and systems integration issues); and
- High-capability applications for the individual (education, digital libraries, in-home medical information).

The crisis management application area bridges all three of these classes. A testbed or technology demonstration that supported distributed training and planning exercises in crisis response, for example, could incorporate modeling of natural and man-made phenomena in real time; secure and reliable communications; interoperability and integration of existing information resources, such as public and commercial databases; and adaptive, user-centered interfaces.

Evolving the High Performance Computing and Communications Initiative to Support the Nation's Information Infrastructure, a comprehensive review of the High Performance Computing and Communications Initiative conducted by the Computer Science and Telecommunications Board (CSTB, 1995a), also supported the notion of emphasizing nationally important applications (what the initiative called National Challenges) to test and guide the development of basic infrastructure:

> Recommendation 8: Ensure that research programs focusing on the National Challenges contribute to the development of information infrastructure technologies as well as to the development of new applications and paradigms. The National Challenges incorporate socially significant problems of national importance that can also drive the development of information infrastructure. Hardware and software researchers should play a major role in these projects to facilitate progress and to improve the communication with researchers developing basic technologies for the information infrastructure. Awards to address the National Challenges should reflect the importance of the area as well as the research team's strength in both the applications and the underlying technologies. The dual emphasis recommended by the steering committee contrasts with the narrower focus on scientific results that has driven many of the Grand Challenge projects.[1]
>
> Testbeds for computing and communications technologies to aid crisis management would support the dual focus on applications and infrastructure by emphasizing the participation of crisis managers and technology experts in limited-scale deployments for training, planning, and to the extent practical, operational missions.
>
> ---
>
> [1] The 1995 CSTB report concluded that the National Challenges defined in the High Performance Computing and Communications Initiative were too broad to offer specific targets for large-scale research, and therefore, "the notion of establishing testbeds for a complete national challenge is premature. Instead, research funding agencies should regard the National Challenges as general areas from which to select specific projects for limited-scale testbeds...." (CSTB, 1995a, p. 59).
>
> The crisis management testbed described by Finding 1 of this current report should be understood as an intermediate step—something larger than a single research project as the 1995 CSTB report implied, but not a complete, nationwide crisis management system.

Finding 1: Crisis Management Testbeds

Testbeds and other experimental technology deployments can enable researchers and technologists to develop and test technologies cooperatively in a realistic application context (see Box 3.3). They can serve as a demanding implementation environment for new technologies and sources of feedback to identify and refine research objectives. Such testing is particularly important in progressing toward deploying national-scale applications, in order to verify theoretical concepts about the scalability of system characteristics, interoperability with other systems, and usability by people in realistic situations —all of which are difficult or impossible to predict in the laboratory.

Test projects and technology demonstrations are under way in most national-scale application areas (NSTC, 1995). However, in civilian crisis management, additional government funding and leadership are required if the research and development benefits of these activities are to be realized. Crisis management is primarily a public service function, led and funded by government agencies. The relatively small operational budgets of federal, state, and local emergency management agencies do not include significant research and development funding. The small size of the commercial marketplace for computing and communications in civilian crisis management, in comparison to areas such as health care, medicine, commerce, and manufacturing, may limit the likelihood of large-scale industry investment in a testbed effort. Greater public investment has been made in the military context, but much of this is related to command and control in warfare, which overlaps with nonmilitary applications only partially. The JWID '95 (Joint Warrior Interoperability Demonstration of 1995, discussed in Chapter 1) military exercise was an exceptional case in incorporating civilian participation in a nonwar crisis response. JWID '96 will not repeat this activity, and no analogous large-scale exercise exists for civilian crisis management organizations to test and experiment with technologies on a similar scale.

Testbeds should provide a context for the participation of crisis management practitioners (such as the Federal Emergency Management Agency (FEMA) and state, local, and nongovernment emergency services organizations) in system testing and development. Application users' input is essential to assess the fit among systems, tools, and the needs of users and organizations and to ensure that technology is focused on usable, practical solutions. In addition, the workshops suggested that testbeds could make a direct contribution to crisis management by supporting realistic training and simulation. Training is crucial to effective crisis management. Workshop participants from the crisis management community made it clear that to be useful, training exercises must be realistic. High-fidelity simulations (including distributed simulation across networks) and field exercises in conjunction with technology demonstrations could help provide this realistic training. Realistic scenario-based "what-if" simulations could also be a useful tool to test operational plans and choices.

1. Establishment of one or more technology testbeds for computing and communications systems in crisis management would be valuable. In these testbeds, government, academic, and industrial researchers should work with application users—crisis managers—to test and validate technologies under research and development by subjecting them to demands in realistic applications, such as training and planning missions for civilian and military crisis management personnel through simulations and field exercises and, potentially, actual field operations.

Finding 2: Studies of Existing National-scale Information Infrastructure

Crises can occur anywhere, at any time, and their management and resolution may require expertise, information, and resources from around the world. The unpredictability of crisis locations and sources of aid leads quickly to the idea that what is needed is an infrastructure that increases the chance of harnessing far-flung information and computing resources on short notice to address a problem, anytime and anywhere they are needed. What are the technical characteristics that make it possible to create or leverage large-scale information infrastructure? How and where should these characteristics be deployed within the information infrastructure to enable ubiquity in the services it supports?[2]

Examples of narrowly focused but successful information infrastructure that functions on a large scale include bank electronic funds transfer systems (e.g., check clearinghouses), automated teller machine networks, airline reservations systems, and airline communications systems such as the Société Internationale de Télécommunications Aéronautiques

(SITA). More general systems include the Internet and applications it supports, including electronic mail and the World Wide Web. What aspects of these systems have led to their ability to scale—in terms of their complexity and the quantity and geographic distribution of their end points—and to accommodate diverse components and evolve over time? These and related questions should form the basis for an exploration of architectural imperatives for national-scale systems.[3]

As the workshops unfolded, it became apparent that many existing, large-scale computing and communications systems could be studied to understand better the general architecture of information infrastructure that can scale successfully to a national or global level. In this finding, it is proposed that an analytical research effort to study the design and operation of these systems could produce valuable results by exposing architectural and design features that contribute to successful operation and might be generalized to apply to many, if not all, information and communications systems.

Many benefits for development of new systems could arise from better understanding of existing systems.[4] For example, in crisis management, access to specialty databases is often crucial; examples include hazardous substance databases, the general databases of the National Library of Medicine, databases at the Centers for Disease Control and Prevention, census databases, corporate human resources records, patient treatment databases, and the like. How are these databases organized and do methods exist that would permit them to interoperate more smoothly in a crisis? Replacing lost local communications resources is another common factor in crisis situations. Are there design principles for large-scale infrastructures that would support integration of rapidly deployed emergency communications facilities with existing resources? Could an electronic "emergency lane" be made to work in some fashion? How can national and regional sensor networks (such as the Oklahoma Mesonetwork and NEXRAD (Next Generation Weather Radar) be integrated easily into other information processing systems? How can this be done on short notice in crisis situations? Relevant research should draw not only on developers or maintainers of major existing systems, but also on communities that typically use the systems.

2. **Existing systems that provide widely accessible computing, communications, and information resources for applications such as electronic commerce, health care support, manufacturing, air traffic control, electronic reservations, and public information dissemination should be examined to identify and understand the critical features that make systems scalable, reliable, and broadly usable. The object is to improve understanding of what information infrastructures are, what components they should include, how they should be structured, what services they should provide, and how they serve the needs of particular applications.**

SUPPORT OF HUMAN ACTIVITIES

In national-scale applications, people are a critical component—humans are "in the loop." Discussions with experts in a number of application domains revealed that although support of people-both as users and as integral parts of the system design—is of primary importance, this need often gets too little emphasis in system designs. To the extent that user roles do receive attention, it is frequently in terms of traditional views of information technology usage in a tool-user relationship, stressing easy-to-use human-machine interface technologies such as speech recognition and graphical displays. These are important and appropriate subjects for continued development; however, independent development of individual technologies will not extend the utility of information technology to the extent that national-scale applications require. Instead, these applications require an integrated approach to system design that recognizes that, increasingly, people and technologies work together as parts of a larger system; both sides provide inputs and add value. The challenge of integration complicates research design and adds to the difficulty of achieving useful results.

An example is an information system that integrates information from sensors, databases, and field workers and supports processing of the information by both computer models and human analysts. People affect the performance of systems both positively and negatively, and system designs should seek to improve and extend human performance. As components of systems, people may provide information; they may direct the activities of computer applications; they may check or verify that decisions or conclusions made by applications are reasonable; they may provide decisions when the applications reach an impasse and cannot make decisions. People may make errors, particularly when under stress. The activities and needs of humans who are not computer specialists, but rather, specialists in their own application areas, must be considered as a component of any system architecture.[5]

Finding 3: Usability

Crisis management requires systems that people can use well without a great deal of specialized expertise. Improving the usability of systems for crisis management, as well as other national-scale applications, faces many challenges. Users are often geographically dispersed and have widely differing skills. Human-computer interaction technologies that will be deployed in national-scale applications cannot depend on high-performance computing and communications being available to all users; technologies must scale across widely varying systems and infrastructures. They must also adapt to a variety of needs. Usability is more than a technical issue. People use technologies that are deployed in the context of a social organization, and usability depends on meeting the user's needs and adapting to the user's capabilities in the context of organizational and social structures and objectives.

Basic preferences of users and their styles of interacting vary greatly depending on domain-specific practices, training, skill level, and the situation. A doctor on rounds may be accustomed to dictating observations, reading charts, and writing prescriptions. Speech recognition, ready access to sensor-supplied patient information and x-rays, and pen-based devices are examples of technologies and devices that, when integrated with patient and health care information systems, not only can enhance the effectiveness of patient care and the efficiency of the caregivers, but also can aid emergency personnel in times of crisis to obtain immediate and current information.

Progress is being made on many of the component technologies and mechanisms, but they remain largely fragmented among domain-specific and situation-specific modes of interaction. There is a need for interactive systems that can be tailored easily and quickly to fit the specific requirements and preferences of users. Research on modeling and understanding user needs in various situations should guide the development of techniques for tailoring interfaces.

In crisis management, situations arise in which transportation infrastructure has been damaged (e.g., during earthquakes). Mobile emergency personnel need very specific information about where to go and how to get there, taking into account the fact that status of local roadways and bridges may be in flux or unknown. They must be able to understand the information quickly; this is where research and experimentation with actual users under stressful conditions can help. In some situations, a brief ext message may be the best way to convey information quickly without leading to confusion; in others, a visual display such as a map or aerial photograph may be appropriate, with the crucial locations highlighted automatically. Moreover, the information flow must be two-way. If a road is not where the database says it should be or a bridge has been knocked out, the mobile user should be able to mark that information on a handheld display and disseminate it to update other users about the situation. Appending a spoken annotation to the data, for example, could be an effective way to enrich the information value added. Implementing such technologies will require new presentation and format standards that link multiple data types easily, while conserving scarce radio bandwidth. The development of standards should be based on clear understanding of what factors matter most to users. Deployment in realistic crisis exercises and actual crises should serve as a means of exposing these factors and quantifying their value.

The granularity and specificity of information needed by different users at different times can vary greatly, as can the capability of users' equipment (e.g., display, storage, processing). Thus, technologies and capabilities to deploy multilayered data views derived from many sources to users with limited resources are needed. How this can be accomplished in one context is illustrated by the University of Oklahoma Center for the Analysis and Prediction of Storms' weather model discussed in Chapter 2: by zooming-in on one area of a larger picture—the state weather map—detailed, very specific information can be developed (e.g., local, time-specific thunderstorms). Mobile users obviously do not have the computation capacity available for this type of weather modeling or even to display the complete results of a regional simulation. Therefore, it would be valuable to be able to focus weather models on the scale and location of greatest interest to the crisis manager and rapidly present the information he or she most needs.

People are error prone, particularly if they are tired and under stress as is common in crises. Depending on the application and instance, human errors may be acceptable or disastrous; in either case, they often are not considered adequately in system designs. Applications should be able to cope with reliability problems caused by errors or failures in any component, including the human component. For example, adaptive mechanisms are needed to elide and compensate for errors and, ideally, to associate and propagate confidence factors with information that other users and applications can interpret.

Systems should also account for the obvious strengths that humans bring to applications—for example, unparalleled inferencing skills and vast arrays of experience and knowledge. Because crises overload people with demands on their time and attention, their strengths should be applied where they are most effective. Formally defining complex problems in a way that identifies where uniquely human abilities are most effective would be a significant advance.

Security is another usability consideration that is particularly important in crisis management. For example, if crisis team workers are setting up a network from the local police radio communications network and a local hospital network, the security mechanisms associated with the combined network must reflect the existing security policies of both parts, yet allow authenticated emergency workers access to appropriate information. This must happen rapidly and may have to be implemented by nonexperts in security, which implies a strong need for highly usable network security management tools.

3. Research is necessary to gain a better understanding of users' needs, capabilities, and limitations in working with computing and communications technologies in diverse contexts. This understanding should be used to develop principles for optimizing the effectiveness of people in the overall performance of applications in which humans and machines work together.

Suggested Research Topics:

- Enabling of natural, interactive communication across a variety of devices and mechanisms used by individuals with a wide range of skills, needs, and financial constraints (which directly affect available computing power, displays, etc.) should be pursued. In building on streams of research already under way in many areas, such as speech and language recognition, graphics and visualization, human-computer interaction, human factors, organizational behavior, and other subdisciplines, a principal multidisciplinary research challenge is to integrate approaches (e.g., multimodal interfaces combining graphics, text, speech, gesture) to meet specific needs and conditions.
- Information management tools are necessary to fuse data from multiple sources, filter information from a potentially overwhelming flood of inputs, integrate it, and present the most crucial information to users under severe time pressures, distractions, and other stresses. These should include a capability to adapt the information management processes in real time in response to user feedback about relevance, timeliness, understandability, and other factors.
- Visually representing the quality of information would be of value to users. It is difficult to represent the quality of three-dimensional-plus-time information (e.g., full-motion video). Error bars may be adequate for showing statistical variance of a data point (such as a sensor input or a casualty estimate) but are less so for indicating the probability that a data point has been misread accidentally or falsified deliberately.
- Visualization of complex data and/or large quantities of information is needed, along with interactive virtual environments that enable users to explore the effects of various assumptions about uncertain or missing inputs and possible future courses of events.[6]

Finding 4: Collaboration

Crisis management is collaborative. Crisis managers interact synchronously (through face-to-face meetings, by telephone, and so on) and asynchronously (through e-mail, voice mail, and information services). They share and organize information, contributing to information stores shared by others, and aggregating and otherwise adding value to diverse pieces of information to enable that information to be a basis for planning, decision, and action. They share work flow, with deadlines for decisions and plans, schedules for actions, and precisely timed operational activities.

In crisis management, collaboration is currently dependent on human transportation—bringing together the key players so they can interact face-to-face—and on the telephone. The most common vehicle for collaboration is the situation room, serving as a physical locus for incoming information and outgoing decisions and plans. This creates delays and inefficiencies, particularly when key players are geographically dispersed or involved in multiple simultaneous efforts. Telephone and occasional video teleconferencing accommodate physical remoteness, but at the cost of reducing the efficiency of sharing and accessing information.

Collaboration, in this context, does not merely include crisis managers sitting in a situation room. It also includes a wide range of other kinds of interactions, from short-duration actions focused on specific decisions to longer-term efforts at gathering and collaboratively integrating information over long periods of time. An open collaboration technology should support the full range.

Research in distributed computing, human-computer interaction, information management, and other areas is beginning to create a foundation for a technology of collaboration, enabling effective interaction across space and time. To support collaboration, research on communications models should address how users communicate with each other.[7] The models must reflect not just speech, but also many other modes of communication. They should include not just the people collaborating, but also the information resources they interact with. For example, extensions to the collaborative perceptual space could include not just video-conferencing, but also a rich synthetic space including visualizations of terrain, buildings, and participants in the crisis response. This kind of shared perceptual space would enable rapid planning iteration, including simulation.

The information space shared by collaborators could include databases, documents, working notes, and other material that crisis managers need to share. Commercial groupware, World Wide Web technology, and some tools associated with the Internet-based Multicast Backbone (MBONE) constitute important initial steps, but there is an unmet need for an Internet-based open-protocol collaboration technology that can support a very broad range of collaborations.

4. **Research is needed to develop concepts for new, open, network-based collaboration tools. Collaboration is essential in crisis response and many other national-scale applications. Although networks are used to support collaboration, currently available collaboration tools are not adequate to suit application needs. Specific tools, technologies, and open protocols to support collaborative efforts could yield significant benefits.**

Suggested Research Topics:

- Common perceptual spaces should be developed that mix video, synthetic (virtual) environments, and information visualizations, to facilitate collaboration among geographically dispersed participants.
- Common information spaces should be developed that support sharing, organizing, and evolving a jointly viewed collection of complex information interactions.
- A virtual situation room, combining common information and perceptual spaces in a collaborative virtual environment, would assist users to gather information, make plans and decisions, initiate actions, and monitor execution.
- Work flow management and judgment support tools (discussed in Box 3.2) are necessary to augment and enhance the capabilities of decision makers by exploiting collaborative problem-solving infrastructures.
- A collaborative problem-solving environment for software development by distributed sets of designers, programmers, and application users could aid more rapid, higher-quality development of software applications.[8]

SYSTEM COMPOSABILITY AND INTEROPERABILITY

Crisis management is a first-rate illustration of the need to rapidly incorporate and utilize a potentially globally distributed collection of communications, information resources, and system components into an application solution. The first requirement is to gain rapid access to information resources of many different types; the second, to integrate these resources into the information that each user needs. Computers and networks can help achieve these goals, but there is a strong need for improved ways to use existing resources (including both old, legacy resources such as city maps and new ones such as the latest satellite imagery from the World Wide Web) and to communicate with existing services. Research aimed at generic tools and services for integrating such systems is discussed in this section. However, scaling to national and global levels requires more than ad hoc approaches, so this section also addresses research toward more forward-looking architectural solutions.

Because crisis management places a premium on information access and integration, workshop discussions focused on composing information systems from multiple sources. However, other types of networked computing systems in national-scale applications—distributed transaction processing and large-scale collaboration, for example—are increasingly interconnected and composed from many parts. The World Wide Web, for example, is a platform across which information, communications, and distributed software applications all work together.

Crisis management requires that information cross heterogeneous interfaces—a translation problem. For example, data files must be translated from one format to another; handheld radio signals must be translated between standards. These translation problems are what is usually meant by "interoperability." Interoperability between systems is crucial for crisis management, but it is not enough. Truly collaborative solutions require the ability to compose or integrate systems. For example, an information system that must perform searches across different databases with different structures requires a closer integration with deeper understanding of semantics than the term "interoperability" often implies.

Semantic composition implies that the user and resource or service have some deeper level of understanding and agreement about an invocation or communication. Semantic composition requires agreement about the meanings of functionality across interfaces. For example, there are different syntactic formats for geographic information systems made by different vendors, such as ArcInfo and MapInfo. Files made for one must be translated to be used by the other, but both share the semantic idea of latitudinal and longitudinal coordinate reference and ideas such as "X is adjacent to Y" and "X surrounds Y."

Finding 5: Focused Standards

In a crisis, many diverse information and communications resources have to be brought together. Because the diversity of resources available over networks is increasing rapidly, they must be linked together by standard protocols and other elements. Without widespread agreement on critical common elements, systems cannot scale up, and national-scale applications will be unworkable.

At the network level, the Internet suite of standards is a particularly compelling example of how well-chosen technical standards create a powerful avenue for interconnection and interoperation. The Internet protocols serve many functions, such as domain name management, addressing, packet transmission, reassembly, and fault tolerance. They are organized into relatively small component elements, enabling users to select particular elements of the Internet suite without having to use the entire set. One example of how this promotes flexibility is that many firewall systems transmit only certain kinds of packets and respond to certain kinds of protocols (e.g., for electronic mail, but not for file transfer). This flexibility has enabled the Internet standards to serve as a de facto basis for many emerging national-scale applications.

In the geographic information systems (GISs) widely used in crisis management applications, a small set of critical commonalities—such as the latitude and longitude coordinate system and depiction of features such as roads and rivers as arcs between points—are accepted widely by a broad community of users and tool vendors. Although translation between different vendors' proprietary data syntaxes is still necessary, these commonalities make interoperation and sharing through GIS possible. For example, the Consequences Assessment Tool developed by FEMA and the Defense Nuclear Agency (discussed in Chapter 1) integrated the outputs of weather models, building-stress analysis models, and nuclear explosion blast-pressure models with databases from the Census Bureau and other sources to project the impacts of Hurricane Emily on neighborhoods in its path. These components had not been designed to interoperate nor were they developed to be part of a crisis management solution. The interoperation was accomplished by accepting a single geographic coordinate system representation.

There are, however, many areas in which multiple standards exist that overlap in function, yet whose service models may not be entirely consistent. For example, a variety of standards apply to different ways of querying and accessing information. Examples include Structured Query Language (SQL; for accessing relational databases), Common Object Request Broker Architecture (CORBA; for accessing structured objects), Object Linking and Embedding (OLE; for accessing distributed structured documents), and American National Standards Institute (ANSI) standard Z39.50 (for digital library information retrieval). Although these services have different functions, there is nonetheless significant overlap among them. Interconnecting these services (e.g., to provide a single client interface for retrieval and presentation of information objects related to a particular application) presents formidable interoperability problems at multiple levels. Existing interoperability solutions are often ad hoc and do not scale well. Although Finding 6 suggests there may be ways to address these problems for current technologies, it is also important to consider new approaches to protocol design in the future that will be more resistant to proliferation and divergence of protocols.

The World Wide Web provides good examples. While there is a wide diversity of clients (browsers) and servers, these diverse components are unified by a set of common protocols and formats, such as HyperText Transfer Protocol (HTTP) for connection management, Uniform Resource Locators (URLs) to name Internet information resources, and HyperText Markup Language (HTML) to describe Web pages. These protocols enable interchangeability and interoperation among the increasingly diverse set of Web tools and technologies. However, the complexity of the HTML language has increased rapidly, and there are now multiple versions in simultaneous use and increasing numbers of browser-specific Web pages.

These examples highlight the need for a "focused standards" approach, in which individual standards are narrowly focused on specific requirements rather than locking in a large, interrelated set of requirements. They should be modular and composable in the same way system components are composable. This facilitates adoption and offers more flexibility for vendors to compete and for integrators to evolve systems. For example, in the Internet, this approach has already led to significant success in achieving interoperation among data communications networks atop which many applications run. Workshop participants and others have argued that the Internet standards are successful because they follow a focused, minimal approach (CSTB, 1994b), with no single standard incorporating all the functions of Internet protocols and services, but instead a large suite (Transmission Control Protocol (TCP), Internet Protocol (IP), File Transfer Protocol (FTP), HTTP, and many others) allowing more flexible interaction with other services and standards than a large set of interlocked "all-or-nothing" standards would have done.

Technology that supports this kind of plug-and-play approach between applications could be called "component middleware."[9] Component middleware technology is just beginning to emerge, and research should aim to accelerate its development. For example, although various developers have produced application programming interfaces (APIs) and libraries of enabling software (such as enabling software for databases distributed across a variety of network substrates), it is not yet apparent that they can interact in a modular plug-and-play fashion on a large scale. APIs introduce constraints on the communications between computing components, and collections of APIs drawn from various sources may not be compatible: even if they allow syntactic interoperation, the semantic meaning across the APIs may be incompatible. Development of general principles for middleware design and implementation that enable the creation of focused, modular standards could contribute greatly to the likelihood of successful interoperation of two components that had not interworked before. It is not yet clear what those general principles might be, but such an approach is clearly more likely than trial-and-error efforts to work well on a national scale.

Two kinds of research are needed: service protocol design and protocol design principles. Service protocol design research focuses on creation of protocols through which new kinds of services can be delivered. Service protocols effectively insulate users of the service from details of implementations and their continued evolution in capability, and they insulate service implementors from details of how the services are used in particular applications. This lessens dependence, facilitates service evolution, and thereby stimulates greater competition for supply of services and consequent growth in capability. Protocol design principles are needed to guide designers of the protocols through which these services are delivered and provide them with some confidence that a new protocol supporting a specific service will interact effectively with other service protocols already in use or emerging. This notion of composition of information services is analogous to concepts related to the composition of software components.

Once services become broadly commercialized, the dependence of multiple organizations on specific protocols and standards makes evolution of those standards difficult. Therefore, early and active involvement by researchers in developing prototype protocols for new service concepts can significantly hasten the acceptance and growth of these new services. Any research program that involves creation of new service concepts should also involve creation, promotion, and evaluation of associated protocols. Researchers developing new concepts for information services should consider protocol design issues from the outset, since the protocol design will be the most likely instrument for scaling up the concepts and moving the technology into broader practice. When new protocol concepts are unencumbered by dependence on specific implementation or platform details (i.e., keeping them focused and minimal), they are more likely to be accepted and to serve as a basis for growth.

5. Research is needed to identify design principles that can yield open standards (such as communications protocols and application programming interfaces) that interact well with other related standards and allow for diversity and evolution. Individual research and development efforts aimed at setting standards should focus on more narrow component functionalities or services, rather than promote aggregation into larger multifunction standards.

Suggested Research Topics:

- Service protocol designs must be developed with the participation of researchers. Areas in which new service protocols are being developed include multimedia (e.g., representation of various multimedia and virtual reality objects, compression, meta-data for indexing and search), database distribution (e.g., distributed queries, object management, agents), collaboration technologies (e.g., video-conferencing, shared virtual spaces, information sharing), and distributed or "migratory" software systems constructed from components available over a network (e.g., the Java programming language). Many of these protocol development efforts are now at the point of commercial standardization, but many others are still in nascent stages, and it is in these cases that participation from the research community can have significant benefit.
- Protocol design principles should be identified. Results of research on protocol design principles would be in the form of design principles that service developers can apply, along with reasoning tools that could be used to assess critical characteristics of protocol design, for example, freedom from deadlock and avoidance of emergent phenomena as use scales up.[10]

Finding 6: Interoperability

The assembly of resources in a crisis includes formation of teams, configuration of communications systems, and interlinking of data resources. It can also include interconnection of tools for planning, decision, visualization and presentation, and work flow management. The diverse players in crisis response are reaping significant benefits from their growing reliance on information technology, and that reliance creates opportunities for effective and rapid integration of resources. However, it also presents significant technical challenges related to interoperability.

For example, in Hurricane Andrew relief operations, enormous efforts were required to incorporate data from county tax assessor registers into the GIS coordinate system being used by relief officials. In the aftermath of the Oakland Hills fires, integration of location data from portable global positioning system (GPS) sensors with paper maps from the local utility proved valuable, but it was accomplished manually.

David Kehrlein, of the Office of Emergency Services, State of California, noted that many of the data gathered at relief stations following the Northridge earthquake, such as names and locations of injured survivors, were very difficult to integrate into a coherent, overall picture. Had the relief stations been using any of a variety of commercial personal computer databases, there would have been the problem of integrating data from those formats into the map-based GIS databases used for command and decision making at higher levels. In fact, many of the data were not even in databases, but in word processors; to officials at the station, that was a "database." These data had to be integrated manually by crisis managers even to yield an accurate overall listing of the locations of survivors, much less to correlate the data with a GIS representation of the disaster area or a logistical information system for ordering and allocating supplies.

Workshop participants identified multimedia data fusion as a valuable research area. This could provide capabilities for integration based on tagging of amateur and professional video with location and time of the images, along with real-time sensor (e.g., atmospheric, seismological) data, keyed to a GIS representation of the crisis area. These data sources are more diverse than in the case of multiple formats for essentially similar database or word processing applications. Significant research challenges relate to the difficulty of fusing data with different formats and access protocols, some with fundamentally different kinds of meta-data (time, location, image resolution, sensor network scale).

The interoperability challenge is particularly acute in crisis management because of stringent deadlines and the inability to anticipate fully the range of resources that must be made to work together. Of course, planning and coordination before crises occur can mitigate problems of interoperation to some degree. However, the planning and coordination have two roles. The first and more obvious role is to reduce the relative proportion of unanticipated cases. The second role, which has potentially far greater leverage, is to create general mechanisms for interoperability and rapid integration that can lower the cost (and uncertainty) of dealing with those unanticipated cases. These factors should certainly be incorporated into the design of any nationally accessible information repository for crisis management, such as the National Emergency Management Information System described by John Hwang, of FEMA. A repository should include not only information for which the need can be anticipated, but also mechanisms for locating, obtaining, interoperating with, and integrating other, unanticipated information sources.

It must also be recognized that information systems and software applications are rarely developed from scratch. Legacy software and databases persist and are the key assets of many enterprises, even in cases where little record remains of the details of their implementation or design rationale. The increasing use of these resources in an interconnected environment raises the stakes for interoperability.

The result of the above factors is that interoperability challenges are increasing, and any technology specifically focused on the problem could have a significant impact. Solutions to interoperability problems need not always be ad hoc, and research focused on this problem may have great impact. For example, wrapper and mediator concepts (see Box 2.4) were initially used entirely in ad hoc ways, crafted by hand to solve specific problems as they arose. Researchers are starting to develop more generic methods (e.g., using data mining and other artificial intelligence techniques) that could lead to tools for semiautomatic generation of intermediate components such as wrappers and mediators. The problem is exacerbated by the increasing diversity of data models and new ways to manage (e.g., name and share) complex object types. However, even very simple approaches to allow sender and receiver to communicate a shared identification of types, such as the Multipurpose Internet Mail Extension (MIME) hierarchy used for structured e-mail documents, have been seen to have considerable benefit. As this report was being prepared, designers of languages for network-centered computation such as Java were still struggling with how to manage the name space for meta-information (types), and groups involved with Web-related technologies were still working out how the name space for Web objects is to be organized.

6. Specific research efforts should be undertaken to develop generic technology that can facilitate interlinking of diverse information resources. National-scale applications present new challenges to interoperability and integration of information resources. Emerging ideas could yield advances such that interoperability problems need not always be met with ad hoc solutions.

Suggested Research Topics:

- While ad hoc approaches to wrappers and mediators have long been in use, generic approaches should be developed that rely on consistent knowledge representation models. Research efforts should be undertaken to assess for what kinds of information resources such generic technologies are feasible.
- Methods are needed to better support the explicit identification and management of meta-information about information resources such as information about types, data models, schemas, and meta-data in networks. Meta-information provides a basis for identifying how information objects are to be interpreted—for example, what coordinate systems are used? What is the quality of the data? Without this basis, reverse engineering is required before information resources can be integrated successfully into composite systems.
- Advances in data fusion of multimedia information from sources such as sensors, relief officials, and amateur citizens are necessary. The usefulness of automatic tagging of inputs (e.g., tagging video images with location and time, as they are generated) should be evaluated.

Finding 7: Integration of Software Components

Rapid response to a crisis may involve integration of applications that were not originally intended to be used together. Crisis management most often involves the need to compose data from different information systems, although integration of software applications such as FEMA's Consequences Assessment Tool (which incorporates federated simulation models and databases) and meso-scale weather models can also be involved. However, the need for composability generalizes to almost every national-scale application area as new systems must be assembled or modified in response to new requirements. For example, design for manufacturing typically involves composing many programs (sometimes numbering in the thousands) that are used for parts of a complex design. These programs are typically legacy systems whose code will never be rewritten.[11] Compounding this problem is the unwillingness of collaborating competitors to share source code.

The ability to compose new solutions out of existing parts is needed to control costs, reuse legacy code, meet competitive time-to-market requirements, solve crisis problems, manage complexity, and reduce programming effort. These depend in part on standards to support interoperability between software subsystems, but more fundamentally on an ability to predict or understand the properties of large software systems.

Currently, composability is often implemented in an ad hoc way. Research on more broadly applicable methods is needed. Solutions are likely multifaceted, encompassing a variety of technologies, including application program interfaces, standards, wrappers, data fusion, cataloging, registering, and common object models. A framework for composability might include a communications model, a distributed computation model, an interface definition language, interface generation tools, protocol or interface translation, a negotiation protocol, and communications facilities among layers of abstraction within and between applications, the infrastructure, and the networks.

The Java language and programming environment serve as a clear example of an environment that was designed from the ground up with these sorts of models, in an effort to ensure composability. To incorporate legacy systems in new architectures is more difficult, and there is a need for an infrastructure with enough standardization to allow interoperation, but not so much as to stifle growth. The ability to address this need likely varies among application areas. For example, civilian crisis management applications are likely to pull together components developed for other purposes. Other industries such as manufacturing are developing application-level architectures for interface specifications, collaboration software, and metacomputing support systems. However, even in this application there are challenges: Lee Holcomb, of the National Aeronautics and Space Administration, noted, "Most companies aren't willing to change their computational infrastructure to work in partnership. So one of the difficulties is . . . trying to get . . . tools to work across different computational platforms through firewalls in each company that are different."

Software composability techniques have the potential to improve the state of the art in a relatively old and intractable problem area, large-scale software system development. Historically, the cost and complexity of large software projects have led to delays in application deployment. More fundamentally, they have also produced systems that do not perform—they do not provide the functionality or reliability required. One avenue toward improving the ability to produce software involves methods for composing systems out of components, including some that may not have been designed to work together, such as legacy systems. This is a very complex problem, requiring advances in many areas.[12]

A very difficult challenge lies in modeling the behavior of composed software systems. It is currently not possible to predict or reason about the functionality, performance, and correctness of most software systems; in practice, the ability of most large software systems to meet requirements is often not determined until the system is built, tested, and tuned. A direction for research that can perhaps address a subset of this problem is the identification and design of composability properties—properties of software components that also characterize systems composed from them. Unless these properties are chosen carefully, it is typically impossible to predict whether a composed system will have the properties of its components. This is why, for example, security or fault tolerance of software systems must virtually always be reevaluated when they are combined into larger systems, even if all the components are individually secure or fault tolerant. Better understanding of composability properties might eliminate this need in some circumstances.

7. To reduce both cost and time, national-scale applications often require construction of software systems from components that already exist or are provided by different suppliers. Research is needed on composability of software systems, including ways of predicting performance, reliability, and other features of composed systems.

Suggested Research Topics:

- Programming models must be developed that facilitate interoperable, composable system construction, as well as prediction and reasoning about the scalability, performance, and correctness (conformance to specified operating parameters) of the resulting system throughout its life cycle.
- Research should address creating a capability for virtual secure groups across different computational platforms.
- Active software objects that users access across networks can provide computing and communications functions across networks, provided they are constructed according to a model that enables them to integrate with each other and with existing applications. For example, the Java language provides a framework of assumptions within which new functionalities can be provided as small, relocatable software components called applets. The ability of these assumptions to remain true when deployed on a national scale is yet to be determined and is worthy of research attention.
- Tools, frameworks, and infrastructure mechanisms are necessary to complement current work on composable, reusable objects. Examples of tools are registries and locators; examples of infrastructure mechanisms are dynamic, distributed linkers and loaders.

Finding 8: Legacy and Longevity

Crisis management places a premium on using known, stable resources and avoiding surprises, because there is no time for training or learning new tools during a crisis. As James Beauchamp, of the U.S. Commander in Chief, Pacific Command, observed (see Chapter 1), "The last [communication equipment] I need in a time of crisis is something I have never worked with before." This statement underscores the premium organizations place on maintaining the usefulness of resources that represent a significant investment of time, understanding, and money over their life cycle and cannot be abandoned lightly. These resources (e.g., radios, maps, databases, word processors) and the infrastructure they rely upon should be designed so they can remain accessible and, ideally, can evolve and incorporate new technologies and services throughout their lifetime. The capacity to adapt and evolve is a necessary feature of the long-lived bodies of information that are central to many national-scale applications.

For example, important text documents containing information needed in a crisis may outlive the word processing or desktop publishing software through which they were created. These documents can always be preserved as images or printer-coded files (such as PostScript), but use of these representations sacrifices access to the content (e.g., for indexing and searching) as well as mutability (to make revisions or to take advantage of new features made available in newer versions of word processing software, for example). Compounding this further is the increasing proliferation of compression and encoding formats that make even basic textual information such as ASCII characters unreadable if knowledge about the formats is lost.

A consistent, lasting way of associating document-type information with long-lived documents would enable, for example, servers to be made available on networks that can interpret documents of various types and, depending on the present task, translate them into other formats, search and index them, or carry out other operations. Network services may help with problems such as the following, as well: How can data from legacy databases be preserved without preserving the actual database system that hosted the data? How can old software be used today, for example, through emulation or translation? Can computer-aided design (CAD) data be managed over the lifetime of a major system without requiring all the CAD tools and their platforms to be preserved as well? Clearly, the more complex the object type, the more challenging this problem becomes. In addition, other legacy assets may create more difficult problems that network-based format translators alone cannot solve. For example, features other than functional interfaces to resources may be long-lived, such as locations and access control lists associated with resources.

The need to support longevity is also paramount in other application domains reviewed in the workshop series. Medical records must be able to follow people as they move through life and must remain useful as technology for creating, organizing, and managing medical information changes.[13] Libraries and other repositories for human expression have similar problems of evolving representations and abstractions of objects (e.g., books, paintings, indices). At Workshop I, David Jack, of the Boeing Company, expressed the same concern in reporting that Boeing must keep available in an accessible form the engineering plans for every airplane they make for the lifetime of that plane, which may be 40 years or more.

The problem in all these cases is that there is a feature of hard copy that must be duplicated in the networked computer environment; a hard copy of a piece of information or expression continues to be usable for the lifetime of the medium. In computer systems, however, the evolution of storage technologies means that the medium may outlast the hardware or software for accessing the information on it, leaving the information inaccessible.

This problem is particularly critical for national-scale applications because these applications and the data supporting them should not be bound to particular software components, computer platforms, data formats, and other technological artifacts that will be outlived by the specific information being managed. Otherwise, application users in the future will be unable to optimize specific technology decisions to meet their needs because they will be shackled by a legacy of old information objects and software. The constraints placed on current technical options by the need to maintain access to technologies developed in the past are the essence of the technological hand-from-the-grave influence that currently restrains the evolution of many large, complex systems, such as the nation's air traffic control systems. An approach to the management of information objects and systems architectures that is based on sound general principles can prevent such constraints in the future.

There are three directions in which further research is needed to address problems of longevity—(1) naming and addressing, (2) resource discovery, and (3) support for evolution. With respect to naming and addressing, a key problem is that information and other resources and services are mobile, and over long periods of time anything that survives is extremely likely to move. For example, network hosts disappear or move to different locations, file systems are reorganized, and whole institutions split, merge, or move. As a result, the situation with respect to URLs, which identify the location of resources in the World Wide Web, is unstable. URLs contain not only the location (including both host name and path name within a host), but also the access method or protocol. Although the widespread deployment of the Web is only a few years old, many URLs have already become obsolete, often providing no recourse to discover whether the information sought has moved elsewhere or is simply unavailable.

One significant direction for improvement, whose requirements were recently defined within the Internet Engineering Task Force, is to separate naming from addressing.[14] This would involve the definition of Uniform Resource Names (URNs), a new type of name intended to be long-lived, globally unique, and independent of either location or access method. These, in turn, are translated (resolved) into URLs as necessary, but it is the URNs that should be embedded in objects for long-term storage, enabling future identification and use. There is still significant work to be done in this domain, because the problems of how to do name-to-location resolution have not been solved. This undertaking is larger in scale by orders of magnitude than the host-name resolution provided by the Internet's Domain Name Service, which is probably inadequate to handle the degree of volatility and mobility needed for URNs because information probably can move much more frequently than hosts. A follow-on problem is that even if a service arises that scales and handles the rate of updates more effectively, in the long run it may well fail or be replaced. Research at the Massachusetts Institute of Technology (MIT; the Information Mesh project) is attempting to address problems of allowing for both a multiplicity of resolution services and an architecture that provides fallback mechanisms, so that if one path to finding resolution fails, another may succeed; this is all very preliminary, however, and more research is needed.

The second part of the solution is to help users find resources. URNs are not intended to be user friendly, but rather computer friendly. Because they should be globally unique, they are unlikely to be mnemonic or to fit into the various naming schemes that suit human preferences. For this, additional resource discovery services are needed, such as keyword searching and similarity checking. There are some significant early efforts in this direction,[15] but there continues to be a need for more sophisticated searching tools, especially as people with less computer savviness become frequent users. It is difficult to build a local naming and search tool that is tuned to particular application domains or to private use. All too frequently these services point to dead ends, such as outdated URLs; the services should be better able to weed out bad data. In a crisis, if a search engine overwhelms the user with an indistinguishable mix of good and bad information, the overall result may be useless.

A third area, discussed further in Finding 9 ("Adaptivity"), relates to the ability of information and other resources to evolve. Although it is desirable for new capabilities and technologies to be employed within equipment and services (e.g., to use new, enhanced interfaces), the evolution must be smooth and easy for people and their applications to adapt to or else the new capabilities may not be used. Application designers cannot know in advance all possible directions for evolution of useful resources, and so to support evolution, applications and infrastructures should be designed to enable applications to learn about and utilize new and evolving resources. The specific research directions implied by this need are discussed in Finding 9.

8. Technological and architectural methods should be developed for reconciling the need to maintain access to long-lived information and software assets with the need to enable application users to exploit new technologies as they become available. Such methods should be applied both at the middleware level and in the architectural design of national-scale applications.

Suggested Research Topics:

- Research is necessary to specify the minimal component services in an information infrastructure that allow for identifying, finding, and accessing resources, and to develop protocols for service definitions that are both minimal in terms of needs and extensible to allow for improved service. Some specific examples following the library analogy are services to help people determine which objects and resources they want (a service like that of a librarian who suggests books), the registration of individual resources (e.g., Library of Congress catalog numbers), the location service (e.g., a catalog), and mechanisms for user authentication and access control policies (e.g., placing books on reserve for students registered in a particular class). Mechanisms to implement these services require, in particular, ways to manage information about how to interpret typed information objects (ranging from documents to data in databases and software components) at the network level.

ADAPTING TO UNCERTAINTY AND CHANGE

A crucial problem faced by all national-scale application areas, but particularly crisis management, is that of dealing effectively with uncertainty in three areas: infrastructure (e.g, networks and network-based services such as naming and addressing), components of integrated solutions, and the nature and behavior of potentially useful resources. Uncertainty and change are involved in all of these areas. In a crisis, changes can produce uncertainty on a scale of minutes: Are the telephone lines in the disaster area down? How soon will they be restored? Change on a longer time scale can also produce uncertainty: Can a firm adapt its new computer system to work with its old databases? These problems highlight the need for systematic, architectural solutions to the problems of adaptivity and reliability. Progress in these specific areas will benefit any application domain that is sensitive to factors such as human errors, overloading of resources, and other unpredictable situations. Indeed, as all application domains grow in scale, these conditions will become more common.

Finding 9: Adaptivity

During and after a crisis, it is critically important that network services and resources be available. This need implies an adaptivity to unusual or extenuating circumstances beyond traditional network operational criteria. Other national-scale application areas could also benefit from increased adaptivity, for several reasons: sharing of network-based resources implies significant fluctuations in demand for and availability of those resources; human errors and system failures are inevitable; and new applications and unusual uses of existing applications can generate entirely unanticipated circumstances. Network-based systems (e.g., communications systems, computer networks, and sensor networks) should be prepared not only to route around points of congestion or failure, but also to adapt to changing availability of resources. Methods for achieving this adaptivity in a crisis are likely to be broadly useful in many domains.

Crisis management demonstrates a number of specific ways in which adaptivity is critical to system design. At the network level, for example, if the local, preexisting network infrastructure is at least partially operational, it may be valuable to integrate it with components brought by the crisis management team. This could involve attaching portable computers preloaded with crisis-related data and software into existing local area networks or connecting predeployed sensors, such as security cameras, into a network deployed for the crisis response.

In practice, identifying and making use of the existing infrastructure are difficult; consequently, relief workers frequently arrive with an entirely separate system whose parts and operation they understand. Yet this approach does not eliminate their problems, because in many cases, multiple organizations arrive, each with its own equipment, networks, and policies for using them (such as access priority and security), making effective integration of all available resources difficult. Adaptivity in this case may reflect the ability to rapidly implement compromise positions where resources owned or controlled by different parties are integrated with agreements about policies for shared use.

Applications that run in uncertain environments also should be designed for adaptivity. For example, if network service is available only intermittently, applications such as shared information repositories and collaboration tools should be prepared to adapt to varying network resources. They should also be reconfigurable or able to configure themselves to take advantage of new or evolving resources. For example, information sent from a crisis command center might be sent to field workers as maps and diagrams when sufficient bandwidth is available, but as text when the bandwidth is reduced. Multiple, distributed copies of databases could be designed to replicate updates to each other (maintaining overall coherence) only when bandwidth is available or to restrict updates only to the highest-priority information such as locations of people needing medical attention. During a videoconference, if congestion occurs, a shift to a lower image resolution could enable the conference to continue. An attractive feature in such circumstances would be support for choice by the users between reduced resolution and fewer frames per second as appropriate to their needs.[16]

A different kind of example is the application that can adapt to changes in the availability of information inputs. Crisis managers must make judgments in the absence of complete data. Judgment support applications (e.g., building damage simulations, logistics planners to estimate emergency supply requirements, map-based evacuation route planners) must adapt not only to statistical uncertainty, but also to gaps, mistakes, and deliberate falsifications in their input data. This requires much more than simplistic interpolation of missing data—it demands an ability to make inferences about what the correct data are likely to be.

Applications also need to evolve and adapt to changes on a longer scale. For example, if simulation-based training programs are designed to train people by providing accurate maps and images of possible crisis locations, adaptivity should enable incorporation of new, better sources for that information over time. Originally, the simulation may use line drawings with altitude designations, later incorporating information from aerial photographs and weather prediction systems.

In crises, it would be especially valuable for applications to discover and exploit automatically, without the need for time- and attention-consuming human intervention, the capabilities of resources whose usefulness could not have been anticipated when the application was written. These might include new objects or services with enhanced functionalities that did not exist when the application was written (e.g., new kinds of environmental sensors); legacy resources that have existed for a long time, but have a structure or form that the application designer did not anticipate having to access (e.g., records of earthquake damage patterns from past years); and resources created for use in a different application area (e.g., architectural designs used to plan evacuation routes during a crisis).

To enable successful use of unanticipated resources in all these cases, continued research should address the question of how applications might learn about and make use of such objects. This problem has two parts. First, the application must be able to learn about the functionality of the new resource, which can be expressed in its type. To find the type of the new resource, the application must be able to ask the resource itself or some other service to identify the type of the resource. Both CORBA and the Information Mesh project at MIT make a first cut at this by requiring that all objects (resources) support a function to answer such a query, if asked. Second, the application may have to import code to access the new type of resource. The importation of code at run time generally is possible only in programming environments that support interpreters, such as the Lisp programming language and its derivatives or Java; importing code at run time to interface into other languages such as C or C++ generally is not feasible. Thus, the problem of utilizing resources of unanticipated types can be split into two research directions, one directed toward protocols for querying objects and the services to support that activity, and the other advancing work in language, compiler, and runtime technologies.

9. Research is needed to increase the adaptivity of networks and applications by providing them with the tools, resources, and facility to function during and after unusual or extenuating circumstances. National-scale applications, especially those supporting crisis management, must be able to function in an environment marked by variability of available resources and of requirements for resources.

Suggested Research Topics:

- Self-organizing networks are those in which the components and resources of the network can discover and learn about each other without the need for a centralized management structure. Self-organizing networks will have less need for human intervention than is otherwise required. There is both theoretical and practical research to be done, ranging from whether such networks can stabilize

themselves, to the protocols by which components learn about each other and the specific kinds of information that components must share to enable self-organization.
- Supporting mobile users and resources is a particular challenge, since the network must be able to reorganize continually. Mobile IP is one way of accounting for mobility by forwarding packets to the user's current location (similar to roaming in cellular telephone systems). However, it introduces latency that is often unacceptable for real-time communications such as voice and video (Katz, 1995).
- Improvements in network management are needed, including tools for discovering the state of existing infrastructure[17] and extensions to current models of network capabilities to reflect such aspects as reliability, availability, security, throughput, connectivity, and configurability. These could enable management tools with new paradigms of merging the access, priority, and security parameters of networks that interconnect with each other during crises in unanticipated ways. One approach might be to develop a priority server that could administer access rights flexibly within a network as users and their needs change during a crisis.
- Methods are needed for reconciling network adaptivity with minimizing vulnerabilities to intruders and other threats. Legitimate actions taken by adaptive self-organizing networks to conform to changes in the available infrastructure may in some cases be difficult for network managers to distinguish from hostile infiltration by an intruder. Significant challenges exist in making secure, adaptive networks that recognize self and do not launch "autoimmune" attacks. Artificial intelligence methods in network management may be a fruitful area for research to meet this need.
- Security should adapt to the mobility of people and changing configurations of networks. For example, how can federal officials arrive in California after an earthquake and provide valid identification recognized by the network without requiring that the infrastructure assign everyone new identities and passwords? How do those officials access useful files from their home offices while in some other security domain? How do the secure domains decide they can trust each other? Research is needed to support composition of security policies across administrative domains and mobility of access rights.
- Crisis managers have a clear need for better tools for discovering what network-accessible resources are available to them in time of crisis. More powerful search and retrieval mechanisms than keyword matching are necessary, as are solutions that allow searching within an unanticipated application domain.
- Rapidly configurable virtual subnets are required that span multiple underlying network resources but provide services such as privacy and access control, as though users were isolated on a private network. Research is needed both to develop the actual protocols necessary to create functional virtual subnets and to provide a clearer understanding of how well virtual subnets can be isolated from broader network environments to

support features such as security, access control, reliability, and bandwidth on demand.
- Application component interface specification and exploration protocols are needed to enable applications to interact with evolving or new resources. There has been some research into interface specifications, but uniformity is lacking. To provide application adaptivity that works at a national scale, either one architecture must be selected (which is unlikely) or protocols must be written to allow negotiation between applications and services of the interface specification language and support tools to be used in any particular case. For example, new protocols would be needed to allow an application that accesses both CORBA objects and OLE objects to discover from objects which kind they are and then use the appropriate model to query the object or resource about its capabilities.

Finding 10: Reliability

The utility of an application or application component often depends on an assessment of its reliability. Maximum reliability is not always necessary; what the user requires is to understand the degree of reliability, to determine whether or not it is within acceptable tolerances, and to decide appropriate actions. In managing a crisis, for example, decision makers must constantly judge the accuracy of the information they are using in making decisions. (They do not necessarily ignore questionable information, but they weigh it differently than more certain information.) Aircraft manufacturers assess the reliability of a subcontractor's part design before incorporating it into an airplane design. Health care workers assess the probable correctness of each item of data about a patient before making a diagnosis or taking action. The quality of inputs, the predictability of events, the validity of simulations, the correct functioning of large-scale applications, and similar factors underlie the quality of information yielded by computer and network applications. These must be understood for people to rely on information and computation technologies in national-scale applications.

To facilitate these assessments for computing and communications systems on which the nation increasingly depends, reliability attributes of system components need to be formalized and exposed whenever possible. This will require research. For example, a crisis response application constructed dynamically from disparate parts must continually predict and assess the reliability of each of its parts. Some of the parts, such as remote computing facilities running a well-tested modeling program, may be assumed by the crisis application to be highly reliable with known probabilities of correctness and measures of precision. More typically, however, many of the components contributing to a crisis management solution do not have such known attributes. This is particularly true if people are part of the system or if untested, previously unintegrated subsystems are used. Furthermore, the nature of the crisis may change a reliable system into an unreliable one through unanticipated scaling problems. Therefore, an important unmet application need is the ability to develop confidence factors based on the reliability of parts of a system.

Assessment of confidence factors can complement other approaches to improving reliability. Many application areas, such as manufacturing, use design and testing processes and redundant subsystems to achieve reliability goals. Adaptive systems, such as those discussed in Finding 9, represent another set of approaches to achieving reliability. Some components of an application solution, however—particularly those involving people—do not have well-defined ways of developing reliability factors. New insights and approaches are needed to improve the reliability of the weak links in a system and, as a separate topic, to capture, quantify, and communicate the reliability status (whether strong or weak) of each component.

The latter topic is particularly important in national-scale applications, which have high public visibility and must provide the public with a high level of confidence that they function correctly and, when they do not, that the problem can be identified and corrected quickly. When an airplane crashes, investigators retrieve the "black box" and analyze recorded data to determine what may have caused the crash, so that steps can be taken to avoid future problems and reestablish public confidence. It would be valuable in national-scale applications to develop a black-box analog (perhaps a set of required procedures) for identifying and correcting errors.

10. Research is needed to enable accurate assessments of the reliability of systems composed of potentially unreliable hardware, software, and people. Consistent methods for evaluating reliability should lead not only to more reliable systems, but also to better ways of using systems in applications, such as crisis management, where absolute reliability is unattainable but reliability factors might be assessable. The ultimate goal of these efforts is to develop measures of confidence in the behavior of systems that support national-scale applications.

Suggested Research Topics:

- A black box technology should be developed for national-scale applications, analogous to that in aircraft, that enables the rapid identification and correction of errors, coupled with procedures for responding to problems that ensure continuing confidence in the viability of the application.
- Basic and applied research in chaotic processes is needed to better understand the reliability of applications in the presence of poor-quality information (e.g., errors, incompleteness, internal inconsistencies). Research might examine the trade-offs between urgency and fidelity of information collection in crises and methods for validating and reconciling poor-quality information.
- To adapt to errors, whatever the source, applications must be robust.

Applications should be self-adapting and have self-describing, self-propagating metrics of component and information reliability. These metrics should reflect the implications of having people as an integral part of applications.
- Reliability attributes should be developed and propagated as meta-data associated with system components.

PERFORMANCE OF DISTRIBUTED SYSTEMS

As the scale of applications grows, not only in the geographical distance between components but also in the complexity of the interrelationships among the components and the utilization of lower-level resources (e.g., networks, processors, memory, storage), the performance of systems that support applications must increase if they are to achieve results rapidly enough to be usable. In addition, the performance of the various infrastructural resources must be balanced to produce effective results.

Finding 11: Performance of Distributed Systems

Crisis management presents an especially challenging set of requirements for balanced performance in both computer systems and networks. Because timeliness is nearly always paramount, extraordinary computing power and network bandwidth are required to ensure that results can be delivered soon enough to be relevant. Moreover, there is rarely time in a crisis to tune software performance, and the easier a computer program is to use effectively, the more likely it is to be used in the stress-laden working environment of a crisis.

Since crises are infrequent and seldom predictable as to place and time, establishing dedicated computing and communications resources is economically impractical. Whatever large-scale, high-performance computing and communications capabilities are made available for responding to a crisis will need to be preempted from less urgent work. The potpourri of data needed to help answer queries and supply input for simulations must be marshaled from its many resident locations as quickly as possible, and high-bandwidth networking must be delivered to the scene for transmission of imagery, including simulation results.

Achieving computer system interoperability, adaptivity, and reliability, especially in connection with a crisis, calls for exceptional computing power and storage capacity. For crisis management, capabilities even beyond those appropriate to ordinary circumstances are required to manage a largely ad hoc and unreliable interconnection of computer systems that were never designed to work together in the first place. The software that makes these deficiencies tolerable adds to the computing burden.

The deployment of computations across networks and the use of distributed and possibly heterogeneous computer systems to address single problems are attractive for crisis management and other national-scale applications.

Increasing the size of many candidate computations to national scale may be impractical because of poor performance. For example, storm and wildfire simulations may perform more poorly as distributed computations than data acquisition and reformatting do. As MIT's Barbara Liskov said, "Everyone knows scalability is important. But no one knows how to show [that] you have it, short of running experiments with huge numbers of machines, which is usually not practical. We need a way to reason about scalability." At every point in the parallel and distributed software design and development cycle, scalability in performance should be treated as a first-class problem.

11. Research is needed to better understand how to reason about, measure, predict, and improve the performance of distributed systems. Crisis management and other national-scale applications demand high-performance systems and tools that balance processing speed, communications bandwidth, and information storage and retrieval.

Suggested Research Topics:

- Current capability to model the performance of systems that are distributed across heterogeneous networks and computing platforms is very limited.[18] Predicting the performance of large, distributed software systems is particularly difficult but would be quite valuable in addressing national-scale application needs. Research is needed to identify what parameters of network, processing, and storage components are critical to systems' ability to meet specified performance criteria, such as capacity and responsiveness, and to develop appropriate metrics for these parameters. Research should include a measurement program to evaluate the ability of models to predict how systems will perform under normal conditions and in crises. These models could be tested, for example, in the context of the crisis management testbeds discussed in Finding 1.

NOTES

1. The reverse, however, is not necessarily true; technologies that have been developed for other domains may not meet the needs of crisis management for coping with urgency and unpredictability.

2. The "where" of deployment includes physical as well as conceptual locations, such as a layer or layers in the technical architecture.

3. The CSTB report observed that the gigabit testbeds—experimental research networks supported under the High Performance Computing and Communications Initiative—supported the concept of large-scale networks offering higher performance than current networks. The examination of existing, apparently successful network architectures advocated in the steering committee's Finding 2 should be seen as complementary to work recommended in the 1995 report's conclusion that "ongoing research in several areas is still needed before a ubiquitous high-performance information infrastructure can be developed and deployed nationwide. . . . [S]uccessful evolution of the nation's communications capability rests on continued investment in basic hardware, networking, and software technologies research" (CSTB, 1995a, p. 54).

4. For a discussion of the relationship between the study of deployed systems and the development of new research directions, see CSTB (1989) and CSTB (1992).

5. A different kind of negative effect that people may have on systems occurs when, in hostile situations such as crime or warfare, they attack systems to harm their performance.

6. Research in scientific visualization aims at permitting computational scientists to observe and understand intuitively the effects of variations in models of phenomena they are studying; see, for example, Hibbard et al. (1994). Extending this sort of visualization into the crisis management context not only requires better models of uncertain phenomena such as mass social behavior, but also challenges the ability to display results meaningfully on equipment of a performance that crisis management agencies are likely to be able to afford.

7. The diversity of organizations with different structures and patterns of working makes it necessary for these communications models to accommodate different modes, when collaboration crosses organizational boundaries as it frequently does.

8. An important feature of the problem-solving environment would be the ability to abstract application requirements and translate those requirements into specifications for software system functionality. Developing such an ability will require considerable research.

9. Middleware provides services within an information infrastructure that are used in common among multiple applications. For a discussion, see CSTB, 1994b, p. 49.

10. The ARPANET, precursor to the Internet, exhibited emergent phenomena related to network control functions that unpredictably produced massive slowdowns in the network. Fundamental design principles to predict and avoid such phenomena in large-scale systems remain lacking.

11. Revisions to code are no guarantee of improvement; managing the proliferation of different versions of the same code is another formidable challenge.

12. Alternatively, Java and similar network-centered models of computing illustrate an emerging, distributed approach to software development. In this approach, developers across the Internet are participating in group development projects using the models of consortia and distributed applications based on multiple interactive Web services. These projects do not look like software development projects in the traditional sense, but they may yield workable, large-scale solutions.

13. In fact, because genetic influences on medical conditions may be understood increasingly, maintaining medical histories longer than a lifetime may become more and more valuable to descendants.

14. Kunze, John A, "Functional Recommendations for Internet Resource Locators," Internet Request for Comments (RFC) 1736, February 1995; and Sollins, Karen, and Larry Masinter, "Functional Requirements for Uniform Resource Names," Internet RFC 1737, December 1994. Both are available on line at http://www.cis.ohio-state.edu/hypertext/information/rfc.html.

15. Examples include the Wide Area Information Service (WAIS) and Harvest, a project at the University of Colorado. There are also a number of searching tools designed specifically for the World Wide Web, such as AltaVista from Digital Equipment Corporation, Lycos, and others.

16. For example, doctors might decide that only the full level of performance is acceptable, whereas medical insurers might opt for lower resolution and professors showing chalkboard diagrams might opt for fewer frames per second.

17. Such tools exist, but are difficult to use and require a higher level of technical expertise than is readily available in a crisis response.

18. Research has achieved some success in one aspect of this problem, that of producing real-time systems. These are systems that can vary their algorithmic approach to a problem in order to converge on a solution by a specified deadline, perhaps sacrificing some accuracy to meet the time constraint. However, much more work is required to generalize this understanding to aspects of performance other than converging before deadlines and to the less well-defined problems characteristic of crises.

Bibliography

Amdahl, Gene M. 1967. "Validity of the Single Processor Approach to Achieving Large-Scale Computing Capabilities." *American Federation of Information Processing Societies Conference Proceedings: Spring Joint Computing Conference*, Vol. 30 . Thompson Books, Washington, D.C.

Andersen, Henning Boje, Henrik Garde, and Verner Andersen. 1994. "MMS: An Electronic Communication System for Emergency Management Organizations." Pp. 34-39 in *International Emergency Management and Engineering Conference: Bridging the Gap Between Theory and Practice: Research and Applications*, James D. Sullivan and Suleyman Tufekci (eds.). The International Emergency Management and Engineering Society (TIEMES), Dallas, Tex.

Beroggi, Giampiero E.G., Laurie Waisel, and William A. Wallace. 1994. "The Role of Virtual Reality Technology in Emergency Management." Pp. 212-217 in *International Emergency Management and Engineering Conference: Bridging the Gap Between T heory and Practice: Research and Applications*, James D. Sullivan and Suleyman Tufekci (eds.). TIEMES, Dallas, Tex.

Brutzman, Donald P., Michael R. Macedonia, and Michael J. Zyda. 1996. "Internetwork Infrastructure Requirements for Virtual Environments." In *White Papers: The Unpredictable Certainty* . National Academy Press, Washington, D.C., forthcoming.

Committee on Information and Communications (CIC). 1995a. *America in the Age of Information: Strategic Implementation Plan* . National Science and Technology Council (NSTC), Washington, D.C., March 10 .

Committee on Information and Communications (CIC). 1995b. *America in the Age of Information: A Forum on Federal Information and Communications R&D* . Compendium of draft white papers for forum, Washington, D.C., July 6-7. NSTC, Washington, D.C.

Computer Science and Technology Board (CSTB), National Research Council. 1989. *Scaling Up: A Research Agenda for Software Engineering* . National Academy Press, Washington, D.C.

Computer Science and Telecommunications Board (CSTB), National Research Council. 1992. *Computing the Future: A Broader Agenda for Computer Science and Engineering* . National Academy Press, Washington, D.C.

Computer Science and Telecommunications Board (CSTB), National Research Council. 1994a. *Information Technology in the Service Society: A Twenty-First Century Lever* . National Academy Press, Washington, D.C.

Computer Science and Telecommunications Board (CSTB), National Research Council. 1994b. *Realizing the Information Future: The Internet and Beyond* . National Academy Press, Washington, D.C.

Computer Science and Telecommunications Board (CSTB), National Research Council. 1995a. *Evolving the High Performance Computing and Communications Initiative to Support the Nation's Information Infrastructure*. National Academy Press, Washington, D.C.

Computer Science and Telecommunications Board (CSTB), National Research Council. 1995b. *Information Technology for Manufacturing: A Research Agenda*. National Academy Press, Washington, D.C.

Computer Systems Policy Project (CSPP). 1991. *Expanding the Vision of High Performance Computing and Communications: Linking America for the Future*. CSPP, Washington, D.C., December 3.

Davis, Larry S., Joel Saltz, and Jerry Feldman. 1995. "NSF Workshop on High Performance Computing and Communications and Health Care," Summary of workshop, December 8-10, 1994, Washington, D.C. Available on line at http://www.umiacs.umd.edu/users/lsd/papers/nsfwork.html.

Dixon, Frank, Frank Gargione, and Richard T. Gedney. 1995. "ACTS to the Rescue." *Satellite Communications* 19(8):27-29.

Drabek, Thomas E. 1991. *Microcomputers in Emergency Management*. Institute of Behavioral Science, University of Colorado, Boulder, Colo.

Droegemeier, Kelvin K. 1993. "Storm Warning: Field Program to Validate a Thunderstorm Prediction Model." Pp. 28-29 in *Projects in Scientific Computing*. Pittsburgh Supercomputing Center, Pittsburgh, Pa.

Federal Emergency Management Agency (FEMA). 1993. *Lessons of Hurricane Andrew*. Excerpts from 15th Annual National Hurricane Conference, Orlando, Fla., April 13-16. FEMA, Washington, D.C.

Fox, Geoffrey C., and Wojtek Furmanski. 1995. "The Use of the National Information Infrastructure and High Performance Computers in Industry," NPAC Technical Report SCCS-732. Available on line at http://www.npac.syr.edu/techreports/html.

Garcia-Molina, Hector, Yannis Papakonstantinou, Dallan Quass, Anand Rajaraman, Yehoshua Sagiv, Jeffrey Ullman, and Jennifer Widom. 1995. "The TSIMMIS Approach to Mediation: Data Models and Languages (Extended Abstract)." Available on line at http://www-db.stanford.edu/tsimmis/publications.html.

Gillies, Douglas. 1994. "Can We Talk? Reviewing Communications Systems After Sudden Cataclysmic Disasters." *Hazard Technology* XIV(4):17.

Government Issue. 1995. "GETS Is Going: AT&T Assembles Emergency Communications Service for NCS." September/October:3.

Hazard Technology. 1995a. "JWID '95: Military, Civilian Experts See Top Systems in Action." XV(2):1, 4. Hazard Technology. 1995b. "Record Hurricane Season Spotlights New Vulnerabilities and Solutions." XV(2):1, 10. Hazard Technology. 1995c. "FAsT Action from FEMA Speeds Hurricane Relief to Virgin Islands." XV(2):11.

Hibbard, William L., Charles R. Dyer, André L. Battaiola, and Marie-Françoise Voidrot-Martinez. 1994. "Interactive Visualization of Earth and Space Science Computations." *IEEE Computer* 27(July):65-72.

Houmb, Ole Gunnar, and Ulf Roar Aakenes. 1994. "A General Environment Information System for Decision Support During Major Emergencies." Pp. 154-160 in *International Emergency Management and Engineering Conference: Bridging the Gap Between Theory and Practice: Research and Applications*, James D. Sullivan and Suleyman Tufekci (eds.). TIEMES, Dallas, Tex.

Institute of Medicine (IOM). 1994. *Health Data in the Information Age*. National Academy Press, Washington, D.C.

International Emergency Management and Engineering Conference: Bridging the Gap Between Theory and Practice: Research and Applications, James D. Sullivan and Suleyman Tufekci (eds.). 1994. TIEMES, Dallas, Tex.

Jensen, Steven J. 1994. "Automated Emergency Management: A Proposal for a Standardized System." Pp. 309-313 in *International Emergency Management and Engineering Conference: Bridging the Gap Between Theory and Practice: Research and Applications*, James D. Sullivan and Suleyman Tufekci (eds.). TIEMES, Dallas, Tex.

Katz, Randy H. 1995. "Adaptation and Mobility in Wireless Information Systems." Unpublished paper available from http://daedalus.cs.berkeley.edu. August 18.

Kvalem, John, and Egil Stokke. 1994. "Integrated User Interface for MEM Decision Support." Pp. 113-119 in *International Emergency Management and Engineering Conference: Bridging the Gap Between Theory and Practice: Research and Applications*, James D. Sullivan and Suleyman Tufekci (eds.). TIEMES, Dallas, Tex.

Landauer, Thomas K. 1995. *The Trouble with Computers: Usefulness, Usability, and Productivity*. MIT Press, Cambridge, Mass.

Lax, Peter D. (chairman). 1982. *Report of the Panel on Large-Scale Computing in Science and Engineering*. Sponsored by the U.S. Department of Defense and the National Science Foundation, in cooperation with the Department of Energy and the National Aeronautics and Space Administration, Washington, D.C., December 26.

Linz, Adrian, and Paul Bryant. 1994. "The All-Hazard Situation Assessment Prototype." Pp. 175-179 in *International Emergency Management and Engineering Conference: Bridging the Gap Between Theory and Practice: Research and Applications*, James D. Sullivan and Suleyman Tufekci (eds.). TIEMES, Dallas, Tex.

Lynch, Clifford, and Hector Garcia-Molina. 1995. "Interoperability, Scaling, and the Digital Laboratories Research Agenda." Report on the Information Infrastructure Technology and Applications (IITA) Digital Libraries Workshop, Reston, Va., May 18150;19. Available on line at http://www-diglib.stanford.edu/diglib/pub/reports/iita-dlw.

Macedonia, Michael R., Michael J. Zyda, David R. Pratt, Donald P. Brutzman, and Paul T. Barham. 1995. "Exploiting Reality with Multicast Groups: A Network Architecture for Large-Scale Virtual Environments." Proceedings of Institute for Electrical and Electronics Engineers (IEEE) Virtual Reality Annual International Symposium (VRAIS), March 11-15, Research Triangle Park, N.C.

Moore, Timothy J., Michael F. Vetter, and Melanie S. Ziegler. 1994. "Simulated Images for Emergency Management Training." Pp. 197-204 in *International Emergency Management and Engineering Conference: Bridging the Gap Between Theory and Practice: Research and Applications*, James D. Sullivan and Suleyman Tufekci (eds.). TIEMES, Dallas, Tex.

Morentz, James W., and David A. Griffith. 1994. "Improving Emergency Planning, Preparedness, and Response with GIS." Pp. 9-13 in *International Emergency Management and Engineering Conference: Bridging the Gap Between Theory and Practice: Research and Applications*, James D. Sullivan and Suleyman Tufekci (eds.). TIEMES, Dallas, Tex.

National Science and Technology Council (NSTC). 1995. *High Performance Computing and Communications: Foundation for America's Information Future*. NSTC, Washington, D.C.

Newkirk, Ross T. 1994. "Information Integration for Emergency Management and Engineering." Pp. 303-308 in *International Emergency Management and Engineering Conference: Bridging the Gap Between Theory and Practice: Research and Application s*, James D. Sullivan and Suleyman Tufekci (eds.). TIEMES, Dallas, Tex.

Office of Science and Technology Policy (OSTP). 1993. *Grand Challenges 1993: High Performance Computing and Communications*. OSTP, Washington, D.C.

Office of Science and Technology Policy (OSTP). 1994a. *High Performance Computing and Communications: Toward a National Information Infrastructure* . OSTP, Washington, D.C.

Office of Science and Technology Policy (OSTP). 1994b. *High Performance Computing and Communications: Information Infrastructure Technology and Applications*. OSTP, Washington, D.C., February.

Office of Technology Assessment (OTA). 1995. *Distributed Interactive Simulation of Combat*. U.S. Government Printing Office, Washington, D.C., September.

Oklahoma State University and University of Oklahoma. 1993. *Oklahoma Mesonet*. The Oklahoma Mesonetwork, Norman, Okla., Summer.

Perry, Walter L., John Y. Schrader, and Barry M. Wilson. 1992. *A Variable Resolution Approach to Modeling Command and Control in Disaster Relief Operations*. RAND Corporation, Santa Monica, Calif.

Proceedings of the 1993 Simulation Multiconference on the International Emergency Management and Engineering Conference: Tenth Anniversary: Research and Applications, James D. Sullivan (ed.). 1993. Society for Computer Simulation, San Diego, Calif.

Proceedings of the 1995 Simulation Multiconference, Maurice Ades and Ariel Sharon (eds.). 1995. Society for Computer Simulation, San Diego, Calif.

Ramsay, Stephen, and Matthew Hilbert. 1994. "MONTY: A Monte Carlo Method for Quantitative Risk Assessment." Pp. 91-96 in *International Emergency Management and Engineering Conference: Bridging the Gap Between Theory and Practice: Research and Applications*, James D. Sullivan and Suleyman Tufekci (eds.). TIEMES, Dallas, Tex.

"Research Priorities in Networking and Communications: Report to the NSF Division of Networking and Communications Research and Infrastructure." 1995. Report of a workshop, Airlie House, Va., May 12-14, 1994. Available on line at http://www.cise.nsf.gov/cise/ncri.

Sawyer, Kathy. 1995. "Increasing the Accuracy of Foretelling Hurricanes' Deadly Turns." *Washington Post*, July 31, p. A3.

Shavit, Yaron, Valerie Lavigne, and Marc Firmignac. 1994. "Integration of Emergency Management Information Systems: Towards a Common Reference Model." Pp. 295-302 in *International Emergency Management and Engineering Conference: Bridging the Gap Between Theory and Practice: Research and Applications*, James D. Sullivan and Suleyman Tufekci (eds.). TIEMES, Dallas, Tex.

Syracuse University and Multidisciplinary Analysis and Design Industrial Consortium (MADIC) Team 2. 1995. "Definition of Requirements for an Aeronautics Affordable Systems Optimization Process (Revision 1)." Draft submitted to NASA Langley Research Center. Syracuse University and MADIC Team 2, December 15.

Vernon, Mary K., Edward D. Lazowska, and Stewart D. Personick (eds.). 1994. *R&D for the NII: Technical Challenges*. Report of a symposium, February 28 through March 1, Gaithersburg, Md. Interuniversity Communications Council, Educom, Washington, D.C.

Wiederhold, Gio. 1992. "Mediators in the Architecture of Future Information Systems." *IEEE Computer* 25(3):38-49.

Xue, Ming, Keith Brewster, Kelvin K. Droegemeier, Fred Carr, Vince Wong, Yuhe Liu, Adwait Sathye, G. Bassett, Paul Yanish, Jason Levit, and Phillip Bothwell. 1996. "Real Time Prediction of Storm-Scale Weather During VORTEX-95, Part II: Operation Summary and Example Cases" (preprint). American Meteorological Society 18th Conference on Severe Local Storms, February. San Francisco, Calif. Available on line at http://wwwcaps.uoknor.edu

Appendixes

A

Workshop Series on High Performance Computing and Communications

WORKSHOP I: AN ASSESSMENT OF HPCC AND APPLICATION NEEDS

AGENDA

Monday, August 15, 1994	
7:30-8:30 a.m.	Breakfast
8:30-8:45	Welcoming Remarks and Introductions
	• Ken Kennedy, Rice University, Steering Committee Chair
8:45-9:45	Relationships: High-Performance Computing, National Information Infrastructure, and the Internet
	• Thomas Kalil, National Economic Council (via video)
9:45-10:30	Technology Status and Directions: Internet—The Once and Future Network
	• David Farber, University of Pennsylvania
10:30-10:45	Break and Informal Discussions

10:45-12:15 p.m.	Applications and Needs in Information Delivery and Services • Daniel Schutzer, Citibank • Clifford Lynch, University of California
12:15-1:15	Lunch
1:15-2:45	Applications and Needs in Medical Care • James Ostell, National Library of Medicine • Joel Saltz, University of Maryland
2:45-3:00	Break and Informal Discussion
3:00-4:30	Applications and Needs in Design and Manufacturing • David Jack, The Boeing Company • Peter Will, Information Sciences Institute
4:30-5:30	Assessment and Discussion of Common Needs • Ken Kennedy, Rice University
5:30	Reception and Dinner
Tuesday, August 16, 1994	
7:30-8:30 a.m.	Breakfast
8:30-9:00	Technology Status and Directions: The Emerging Global Digital Library (Including Mosaic Demonstration) • Larry Smarr, National Center for Supercomputing Applications
9:00-9:30	Technology Status and Directions: Computer Architectures and Hardware • John Hennessy, Stanford University • Burton Smith, Tera Computer Company
9:30-9:45	Break and Informal Discussions
9:45-10:45	Technology Status and Directions: Operating Systems • Brian Bershad, University of Washington Distributed and Heterogeneous Systems • Clifford Neuman, University of Southern California • Karen Sollins, Massachusetts Institute of Technology

10:45-11:00	Break and Informal Discussions
11:00-11:45	Technology Status and Directions: Computing Environments
	• Frances Allen, IBM T.J. Watson Research Center Languages, Compilers, and Application Development Tools
	• Geoffrey Fox, Syracuse University
	• Ken Kennedy, Rice University
11:45-1:00 p.m.	Lunch
1:00-2:15	Middle Layer Services and Application Needs
	• William Scherlis, Carnegie Mellon University
	• Randy Katz, Defense Advanced Research Projects Agency
2:15-2:30	Break and Informal Discussions
2:30-3:45	Privacy, Authentication, and Security in Network Commerce
	• Clifford Neuman, University of Southern California
	• Karen Sollins, Massachusetts Institute of Technology
3:45-4:00	Break and Informal Discussions
4:00-5:00	Application Needs and Research Directions
	• Ken Kennedy, Rice University
5:00-7:30	Dinner
Wednesday, August 17, 1994	
7:30-8:30 a.m.	Breakfast
8:30-9:30	Building the Needed Infrastructure
	• Leonard Kleinrock, University of California, Los Angeles

9:30-10:15	Government Applications of the Developing Infrastructure • Eliot Christian, U.S. Geological Survey
10:15-10:30	Break and Informal Discussions
10:30-11:45	Overall Application Critique of Technical Status and Directions • Geoffrey Fox, Syracuse University
11:45-12:30 p.m.	Summation, Future Activities, and Workshop Closing • Ken Kennedy, Rice University
12:30	Lunch and Adjourn

Participants

 Robert Aiken, Department of Energy
 Frances Allen, IBM T.J. Watson Research Center
 Brian Bershad, University of Washington
 Eliot Christian, U.S. Geological Survey
 David Farber, University of Pennsylvania
 Geoffrey Fox, Syracuse University
 Dennis Gannon, Indiana University
 Robert Haar, General Motors Research Laboratories
 Stephen Haynes, West Publishing Company
 John Hennessy, Stanford University
 David Jack, The Boeing Company
 Richard Johnson, Booz-Allen & Hamilton
 Thomas Kalil, National Economic Council
 Randy Katz, Defense Advanced Research Projects Agency
 Ken Kennedy, Rice University
 Leonard Kleinrock, University of California, Los Angeles
 Clifford Lynch, Office of the President, University of California
 Robert Neches, Defense Advanced Research Projects Agency
 Clifford Neuman, University of Southern California
 James Ostell, National Library of Medicine
 Judith Ozbolt, University of Virginia
 Merrell Patrick, National Science Foundation
 Friedrich Prinz, Carnegie Mellon University
 Al Rosenheck, Congressional Fellow
 Paul Rubbert, Boeing Commercial Airplane Group
 Joel Saltz, University of Maryland
 William Scherlis, Carnegie Mellon University

Daniel Schutzer, Citibank
Henry D. Shay, Lawrence Livermore National Laboratory
Larry Smarr, University of Illinois at Urbana-Champaign
Burton Smith, Tera Computer Company
Karen Sollins, Massachusetts Institute of Technology
Paul Tang, Northwestern Memorial Hospital
John Toole, Defense Advanced Research Projects Agency
Jan Tulinius, Rockwell International
J. Douglas Tygar, Carnegie Mellon University
Peter Will, University of Southern California
William Wulf, University of Virginia
Paul Young, National Science Foundation

WORKSHOP II: HPCC AND CRISIS MANAGEMENT

Agenda

Monday, June 12, 1995	
7:30-8:30 a.m.	Breakfast
8:30-9:00	Opening Remarks
	• Ken Kennedy, Rice University, Steering Committee Chair
	• John Hwang, Federal Emergency Management Agency
9:00-10:00	Damage Assessment and Response Modeling
	• Robert Kehlet, Defense Nuclear Agency
10:00-10:15	Break
10:15-11:15	Sensors, Data, and Modeling
	• Kelvin Droegemeier, Center for Analysis and Prediction of Storms, University of Oklahoma
11:15-12:15 p.m.	Interoperability, Command and Control
	• Don Eddington, Naval Research and Development Laboratory
12:15-1:15	Lunch

1:15-2:45	Field Applications: Emergency Response and Instant Administration • David Kehrlein, Office of Emergency Services, State of California • James Beauchamp, Deployable Joint Task Force Augmentation Cell, CINCPAC
2:45-3:00	Discussion and Charge to Working Groups • Steering Committee
3:00-3:15	Break
3:15-5:30	Working Group Sessions 1. Data and Communications: Sensors, Networks, Interconnectivity, Security • Moderators: Vinton Cerf, MCI Telecommunications Karen Sollins, Massachusetts Institute of Technology 2. Analysis and Computation: Modeling and Simulation, Validation, Integration • Moderators: Ken Kennedy, Rice University Burton Smith, Tera Computer Company 3. Interpretation and Action: Decision Support, Human Interaction, Information Management • Moderators: Frances Allen, IBM T.J. Watson Research Center Geoffrey Fox, Syracuse University
5:30	Reception and Dinner
Tuesday, June 13, 1995	
7:30-8:30 a.m.	Breakfast
8:30-9:30	Preliminary Reports from Working Groups • Nature of the Crisis Management Information and Communications Problem • Unmet Needs of the Crisis Management Community in Computing and Communications • Emerging Opportunities for New Technology Development

9:30-12:00 p.m.	Working Group Sessions
12:00-1:00	Lunch
1:00-2:30	Working Group Sessions
2:30-2:45	Break
2:45-4:00	Final Reports by Working Groups • Refined Statement of Unmet Computing and Communications Needs • Possibilities for (A) Incremental Improvements and (B) "Breakthrough" Applications Enabled by Advances in Computing and Communications Power, Integration, Ease of Use, and Wide Availability • High-potential HPCC Research Opportunities to Meet Crisis Management Needs
4:00-5:15	Discussion, Synthesis, and Assignment of Research Priorities
5:15-5:30	Next Steps and Adjourn

Participants

W. Richards Adrion, University of Massachusetts
Frances Allen, IBM T.J. Watson Research Center
David Austin, Edgewater, Md.
Madeleine Bates, BBN Systems and Technologies
James Beauchamp, U.S. CINCPAC (U.S. Commander in Chief, Pacific Command)
Donald Brown, University of Virginia
Bernd Bruegge, Carnegie Mellon University
William Buzbee, National Center for Atmospheric Research
Vinton G. Cerf, MCI Telecommunications
Eliot Christian, U.S. Geological Survey
Nicole Dash, University of Delaware
Larry Davis, University of Maryland
Kelvin Droegemeier, University of Oklahoma
Daniel Duchamp, Columbia University
Don Eddington, Naval Research and Development Laboratory
Richard Entlich, Institute for Defense Analyses
Robert Fleming, Naval Research and Development Laboratory

Geoffrey Fox, Syracuse University
Peter Freeman, Georgia Institute of Technology
Victor Frost, University of Kansas
Roger Ghanem, State University of New York, Buffalo
Egill Hauksson, California Institute of Technology
Charles J. Henkin, CNA Corporation
William Hibbard, University of Wisconsin, Madison
John Hwang, Federal Emergency Management Agency
Rajeev Jain, University of California, Los Angeles
Robert Kehlet, Defense Nuclear Agency
David Kehrlein, Office of Emergency Services, State of California
Richard A. Kemmerer, University of California, Santa Barbara
Ken Kennedy, Rice University
Paul Kowalski, Unisys Corporation
David Maier, Oregon Graduate Institute
William Mark, Lockheed Martin Palo Alto Research Laboratories
Lois Clark McCoy, National Institute of Urban Search and Rescue
Walter McKnight, National Communications System
Alan McLaughlin, Massachusetts Institute of Technology
Mary Fran Myers, University of Colorado
Robert Neches, Defense Advanced Research Projects Agency
Peter G. Neumann, SRI International
Judith Ozbolt, University of Virginia
Ira Richer, MITRE Corporation
Steven Roa, Naval Research and Development Laboratory
Joel Saltz, University of Maryland
Charles A. Slocomb, Los Alamos National Laboratory
Burton Smith, Tera Computer Company
Jonathan Smith, University of Pennsylvania
Steven J. Smith, National Center for Atmospheric Research
Karen Sollins, Massachusetts Institute of Technology
Joseph Stewart II, MITRE Corporation
Stuart Thorson, Syracuse University
Jonathan Turner, Washington University
Richard Watson, Lawrence Livermore National Laboratory
Jon Webb, Carnegie Mellon University

WORKSHOP III: HPCC RESEARCH AND APPLICATION NEEDS

Agenda

Thursday, August 24, 1995	
7:30-8:30 a.m.	Breakfast
8:30-8:45	Opening Remarks
	• Ken Kennedy, Rice University, Steering Committee Chair
8:45-9:45	Application Needs for Advances in HPCC
	• Banking and Commerce, Daniel Schutzer, Citibank
	• Health Care, Joel Saltz, University of Maryland
	• Manufacturing, Geoffrey Fox, Syracuse University Presenters will draw from Workshop I and other efforts to establish a baseline for further discussion, focusing on what appears most essential today.
9:45-10:45	Crisis Management Application Needs
	• Overview of Workshop II Findings, Ken Kennedy
	• Crisis Scenarios, Geoffrey Fox; Vinton Cerf,
	• MCI Telecommunications Presentation of one or two crisis scenarios to help guide subsequent discussions. Focus is on identifying problems that stretch the capabilities of HPCC technologies.
10:45-11:00	Break
11:00-12:30 p.m.	Research Issues: Computation and Analysis
	• Discussion Leaders: Burton Smith, Tera Computer Company; Ken Kennedy Issues may include, among others: modeling complex phenomena; multidisciplinary simulation and optimization; distributed information systems with prioritized data caching based on meta-data; database verification through simulation and parameter identification; scalable systems; simulation applications in training and planning.

12:30-1:30	Lunch
1:30-3:00	Research Issues: Communications and Sensors • Discussion Leaders: Karen Sollins, Massachusetts Institute of Technology; Vinton Cerf Issues may include, among others: self-configuring, rapidly deployable networks; architectures and network management (e.g., distributed systems with smart sensors and portable workstations; centralized systems with high-bandwidth links); security; reliability; protecting intellectual property; data compression; and other efficiency techniques.
3:00-3:15	Break
3:15-4:45	Research Issues: Interpretation and Action • Discussion Leaders: Frances Allen, IBM T.J. Watson Research Center; Geoffrey Fox; William Scherlis, Carnegie Mellon University Issues may include, among others: adaptive user interfaces (flexible, easy to use by nonexperts during crises); multisource and multimedia data fusion; data mining; knowledge extraction and judgment; computer-supported collaborative work.
4:45-5:30	Synthesis and Next Steps • Ken Kennedy • HPCC Agency Representatives Generalizability of workshop findings across domains and sectors; ordering of findings; research and other possible action items for DARPA and other agencies; relationship of HPCC-based activity to broader initiatives in the federal government and in application domains.
5:30	Reception and Dinner

Participants

Duane Adams, Defense Advanced Research Projects Agency
Robert Aiken, U.S. Department of Energy
Frances Allen, IBM T.J. Watson Research Center

Yigal Arens, University of Southern California
William Arms, Corporation for National Research Initiatives
Donald Brown, University of Virginia
Vinton G. Cerf, MCI Telecommunications
Eliot Christian, U.S. Geological Survey
David D. Clark, Massachusetts Institute of Technology
Stephen Cross, Carnegie Mellon University
Walter C. Ermler, U.S. Department of Energy
David Farber, University of Pennsylvania
Geoffrey Fox, Syracuse University
Dennis Gannon, Indiana University
David Gunning, Defense Advanced Research Projects Agency
Lee Holcomb, National Aeronautics and Space Administration
John Hwang, Federal Emergency Management Agency
David Kehrlein, Office of Emergency Services, State of California
Ken Kennedy, Rice University
Thomas Kraay, Booz-Allen & Hamilton Inc.
Barbara Liskov, Massachusetts Institute of Technology
Teresa F. Lunt, Defense Advanced Research Projects Agency
Clifford Lynch, Office of the President, University of California
Lois Clark McCoy, National Institute for Urban Search and Rescue
Clifford Neuman, University of Southern California
Joel Saltz, University of Maryland
William Scherlis, Carnegie Mellon University
Daniel Schutzer, Citibank, N.A.
Allen Sears, Defense Advanced Research Projects Agency
Burton Smith, Tera Computer Company
Karen Sollins, Massachusetts Institute of Technology
Mary Vernon, University of Wisconsin, Madison
John Wroclawski, Massachusetts Institute of Technology
William Wulf, University of Virginia
Michael J. Zyda, Naval Postgraduate School

B
Background-HPCCI and NII

The federal High Performance Computing and Communications Initiative (HPCCI) was the culmination of a decade of activity focused on building truly high performance computing and communications tools and putting them in the hands of science and engineering users within the United States. This activity dates back to the Lax report (Lax, 1982) and included the founding of the National Science Foundation supercomputer centers in the mid-1980s and the establishment of high-performance computing centers by other agencies as well. The HPCCI developed out of discussions within federal agencies in the late 1980s, leading to the publication of a program strategy in 1987 and a program plan in 1989.

The HPCCI was formalized in the fiscal year (FY) 1992 President's budget and by the High Performance Computing Act of 1991 (P.L. 102-94) authorizing a 5-year program in high-performance computing and communications. This legislation affirmed the interagency character of the HPCCI, assigning broad research and development emphases to the 10 federal agencies that were then participating in the program, without precluding the future participation of other agencies.

One major goal of the HPCCI was to provide the computational and communications infrastructure needed to attack truly difficult problems in science and engineering, known as Grand Challenges. The Grand Challenges identified in the first annual program plan, known as the Blue Book (OSTP, 1993), were the following:

- Forecasting severe weather events,
- Cancer gene research,
- Predicting new superconductors,
- Simulating and visualizing air pollution,
- Aerospace vehicle design,
- Energy conservation and turbulent combustion,
- Microelectronics design and packaging, and
- Earth biosphere research.

In subsequent years, other Grand Challenge areas were added. By focusing on problem solving, the HPCCI greatly improved the interaction between technology developers and end users of the technology. That interaction accelerated progress in the development and deployment of high-performance systems, networks, software, and associated usability technologies.

However, one criticism of the HPCCI was that although the focus on Grand Challenges was very important to science and engineering and provided valuable balance to the program, its impact on the average citizen was very indirect (CSPP, 1991). In response to this criticism, the initiative was extended in the FY 1995 Blue Book (OSTP, 1994a) to include research on the development and application of a national information infrastructure (NII) that would leverage technologies and applications associated with elements of the HPCCI. In addition, it extended the application focus to include several National Challenges, which address critical needs of our society and can benefit from high-performance computing and communications and NII research. The National Challenges can be viewed as national-scale applications. The National Challenges listed in the FY 1996 Blue Book (NSTC, 1995) included education and lifelong learning, digital libraries, health care, manufacturing, electronic commerce, environmental monitoring, energy management, civil infrastructure management, and public access to government information. A 1994 report on information infrastructure technology and applications (OSTP, 1994b)—an HPCCI component—notes crisis management as an additional National Challenge.

C

Acronyms and Abbreviations

ACTS	Advanced Communications Technology Satellite
ANSI	American National Standards Institute
API	Application programming interface
ASCII	American Standard Code for Information Interchange
ASOP	Affordable Systems Optimization Process
ATM	Asynchronous transfer mode; Automated teller machine
C^4I	Command, control, communications, computing, and intelligence
CAD	Computer-aided design
CAPS	Center for the Analysis and Prediction of Storms
CFD	Computational fluid dynamics
CIC	Committee on Information and Communications
CINCPAC	Commander in Chief, Pacific Command
CORBA	Common Object Request Broker Architecture
CSTB	Computer Science and Telecommunications Board
CT	Computerized tomography
DARPA	Defense Advanced Research Projects Agency
DOD	Department of Defense
ECG	Electrocardiogram
EDI	Electronic data interchange
ERLink	Emergency Response Link

FCC	Federal Communications Commission
FEMA	Federal Emergency Management Agency
FTP	File Transfer Protocol
GETS	Government Emergency Telecommunications Service
GII	Global information infrastructure
GIS	Geographic information system
GPS	Global positioning system
HF	High frequency
HPCCI	High Performance Computing and Communications Initiative
HPF	High Performance Fortran
HTML	HyperText Markup Language
HTTP	HyperText Transfer Protocol
IETF	Internet Engineering Task Force
IP	Internet Protocol
I-WAY	Information Wide-Area Year
JTF	Joint task force
JWID	Joint Warrior Interoperability Demonstration
LAN	Local area network
MAD	Multidisciplinary analysis and design
MBONE	Multicast Backbone
MIME	Multipurpose Internet Mail Extension
MIT	Massachusetts Institute of Technology
MLP	Multilevel precedence
MPI	Message passing interface
MRI	Magnetic resonance imaging
NASA	National Aeronautics and Space Administration
NCS	National Communications System
NEXRAD	Next Generation Weather Radar
NII	National information infrastructure
NI/USR	National Institute for Urban Search and Rescue
NOAA	National Oceanic and Atmospheric Administration
NSF	National Science Foundation
OLE	Object Linking and Embedding

PC	Personal computer
PDES/STEP	Product Data Exchange using the Standard for the Exchange of Product model data
PIN	Personal identification number
R&D	Research and development
RFC	Request for Comments (Internet)
SITA	Société Internationale de Télécommunications Aéronautiques
SQL	Structured Query Language
TCP	Transmission Control Protocol
TSIMMIS	The Stanford-IBM Manager of Multiple Information Sources
UAV	Unmanned aerial vehicle
URL	Uniform Resource Locator
URN	Uniform Resource Name
VHF	Very high frequency
VRML	Virtual Reality Modeling Language
VSAT	Very small aperture terminal
WAIS	Wide Area Information Service
WWW	World Wide Web